DISABLED PEOPLE AND SOCIAL POLICY

LONGMAN SOCIAL POLICY IN MODERN BRITAIN

Series Editor:
Jo Campling

Published Titles:
The Personal Social Services
Robert Adams

Health Policy and the NHS
Judith Allsop

Equal Opportunities and Social Policy
Barbara Bagilhole

Responding to Poverty
Saul Becker

Housing Problems and Policies
Brian Lund

Crime and Criminal Justice Policy
Tim Newburn

Foundations of the Welfare State
Pat Thane

Older People in Modern Society
Anthea Tinker

Forthcoming Titles:
New Directions in Educational Policy
Paul Lodge

Lone Mothers
Jane Millar

Social Policy and Privatisation
Mark Drakefield

LONGMAN SOCIAL POLICY IN BRITAIN SERIES

Disabled People and Social Policy: From Exclusion to Inclusion

Michael Oliver and Colin Barnes

LONGMAN

London and New York

Addison Wesley Longman Limited
Edinburgh Gate
Harlow
Essex CM20 2JE
United Kingdom
and Associated Companies throughout the world

Published in the United States of America
by Addison Wesley Longman, New York

First published 1998

ISBN 0 582 25987 8

Visit Addison Wesley Longman on the World Wide Web at
http://www.awl-he.com

British Library Cataloguing-in-Publication Data

A catalogue record for this book is available from the British Library

Library of Congress Cataloging-in-Publication Data

Oliver, Michael, 1945–
    Disabled people and social policy from exclusion to inclusion /
Mike Oliver and Colin Barnes.
        p. cm. — (Longman social policy in Britain series)
    Includes bibliographical references and index.
    ISBN 0–582–25987–8
    1. Handicapped—Government policy—Great Britain. 2. Handicapped—
Great Britain—Social conditions. 3. Handicapped—Great Britain—
Economic conditions. 4. Great Britain—Social policy. 5. Great
Britain—Economic policy. I. Barnes, Colin, 1945– . II. Title.
III. Series.
HV1559.G6046 1998
362.4′0456′0941—dc21   98–20663
                                                                          CIP

Set by 35 in 10/11pt Times
Printed in Malaysia, TCP

Promises Like Stairs

Your promises like stairs
Climb high into the sky
Blocking our progress
By confusing truth with lie

You promised the Earth
Then claim we misheard
Now what you're saying
Sounds quite absurd

Your promises like stairs
Lead nowhere fast
Your talk of civil rights
How long will it last?

You promise a cure
For Capitalism's ills
But we're the ones
Expected to take the bitter pills

Capitalism disables
And stairs do too
We promise to removal all disabling barriers
Will that include YOU?

Bob Finlay

CONTENTS

FOREWORD

By the summer of 1972, our minds were made up. One way or another we were going to set up home together. Our situation was typical: one of us at home with an elderly carer, the other in a residential institution. In the wake of the Chronically Sick and Disabled Persons Act, politicians were saying we were now in a 'new era' of integration for the disabled and policy-makers were talking about 'community care'. All we needed was an accessible house, a few gadgets and enough personal assistance to make out. But in the real world things were very different. When we tried to make headway, we found there was next to no accessible rented accommodation. Mortgage lenders thought two disabled would-be borrowers on benefit weren't a very attractive proposition. Home help services were rudimentary; the ILF and Direct Payments hadn't been thought of. We were soon struggling.

We were in the same position as most other disabled people. Finding helpful information was like looking for a needle in a haystack. The nation's housing stock was designed for and controlled by non-disabled people who, for the most part, seemed to want to keep it that way. The shops were overflowing with technical gadgets to make the lives of able-bodied people easier, but 'technical aids for the disabled' were guarded jealously by professional gatekeepers from different authorities. The built environment was to disabled people what an assault course is to the average commando. The national stock of accessible public transport consisted of little more than a few Sunshine Coaches and an Ambulance Service that refused to carry the one thing that gave chair users some sense of freedom, mobility and independence – their wheelchairs.

When we sat scanning the pages of the *Guardian* on 20 September that year, we were stuck for a solution to what was, for most people, a pretty everyday ambition. We didn't know it then, of course, but several years of struggle lay ahead before we would move into a home of our own. Nor did we guess, as we read a letter from someone called Paul Hunt on that day's correspondence page, that we were indeed at the start of a new era – albeit not quite the kind of new era Alf Morris MP had in mind as he talked up his so-called 'charter for the disabled', the Chronically Sick and Disabled Persons Act.

We needed to find an answer to our problems but, at that point, we seemed either to be dealing with sympathetic people who couldn't help, or unsympathetic people who wouldn't. The solutions to our needs were technically simple, but agencies seemed to have no authority to act, or there was no policy, or precedent, or money, or we were already adequately accommodated and thus they couldn't help. The message was that we were being a bit unrealistic, people like us needed to be properly cared for and we would be better off dropping the idea. Such was the power of the prevailing hegemony of ideas, we were at risk of believing they might be right.

In his letter, Paul Hunt was calling disabled people to consider what changes in society were needed if disability was 'to be eradicated or to become no bar to full social participation'. It chimed perfectly, not only with our own frustrations, but also with the experiences of other disabled people who went on with Paul to form the Union of the Physically Impaired against Segregation. Through discussion and analysis, the UPIAS members eventually redefined disability in terms of social exclusion and thus as a particular form of social oppression.

For us, personally, this process helped to clear away a lot of the confusion in our minds, although the process of clearing away the barriers to our ambitions took much longer. It was 26 September 1976 before we were finally able to move into a flat in the Grove Road housing scheme. Something many non-disabled people expect to conclude in a few weeks or months, took us four years.

The broader sociopolitical, historical and cultural context in which this brief tale was played out, is described and explained in this book. Our own little story is a tale that has been, and will no doubt continue to be played out by many other disabled people. Some will achieve their objectives, but many will remain unfulfilled while ever the unnecessary, wasteful and oppressive barriers in society remain in place. Our reference to it here, at once connects real lives with spare but telling text and serves to reinforce the book's early point, that the stuff of intellectual enquiry and academic discourse has real purpose only when it is applied to the concrete task of overcoming disability.

This is a book that is given real strength by the authors' commitment. They make plain their own role as intellectual activists with disabled people in collective action against oppression: describing, interpreting and feeding the conscious self-awareness of an unfolding social movement. It is a timely book, coming as it does at a time of significant political change in which the need to transform welfare looms large and on which they make their own position clear. By this means, they strengthen and develop further the potent blend of social action and social analysis which has been a powerful force running through the disabled people's movement since the early 1970s.

In our view, this is the vital spark which has released in disabled people the creative energy, the ideas and the practical solutions that have the potential to put flesh on the vision of an inclusionary society. Colin Barnes and Michael Oliver's book at once draws on and feeds into this social vision, sketching in a positive role for a form of welfare which enables and supports disabled people's status as equal citizens with full and enforceable civil rights. Set firmly in the realities of late-twentieth century Britain, this book will be seen as the essential introductory text in this field.

Ken and Maggie Davis

ACKNOWLEDGEMENTS

We would like to thank all those disabled people all over the world who have been involved in the struggle to live the life they choose rather than the one others have chosen for them. They have taught and inspired us.

Personally we would like to thank Hil and Joy for being our constant companions in our own struggles to live the lives we choose and their forbearance during our other struggle to produce this book.

Finally, our gratitude goes to Sylvia Furness and Marie Ross for their own struggles to turn chaos into a publishable manuscript, and to Bob Finlay for permission to reproduce the poem 'Promises Like Stairs'.

Michael Oliver and Colin Barnes

INTRODUCTION

When we were first asked to write this book our aim was to provide a textbook which would serve as a basic introduction to the key issues in disability and social policy and we intended to provide a summary of writings on disability which have emerged in recent years in order to clarify our current state of knowledge. As we set about our task, it became increasingly clear that it would not be possible to complete the task in a summative way as originally intended, because knowledge in both areas is becoming increasingly complex and contested.

Instead, we eventually decided that while we wanted to produce a book which would remain a key introductory text accessible to all with an interest in the area, we nevertheless had to stamp it with our own view on the issues to be discussed. In so doing we felt the need to be clear and explicit about our own position and, hence, the challenge we pose to the work of others.

For us, recent developments in social and sociological theory and their impact on disability studies have given rise to a number of concerns. In particular the current fashion for what we shall call 'post' theorising, whether it be termed 'postmodernist', 'post-structuralist' or 'post-fordist', has tended to play down the materiality of disabled people's lives. From sociologies of the body through cultural studies of 'disability' representations to explorations of the individual experiences of impairment, the idea that the world is somehow constructed through discourse alone has become predominant.

While this is rightly part of the story, for us, it provides only a limited analysis which, in many ways, obscures the very meaning of disability as defined by disabled people themselves and, most importantly, its impact on their daily lives, whether it be economic, political or social. For this reason, we have no intention of abandoning the analysis of history, social structure and collective action in favour of the further development of various and, in the main, benign discourses or social constructions of disability. Indeed, at the end of the social policy line for many disabled people are issues of survival; of life and death. This is especially the case for the majority of those in several of the 'developing' nations of the majority world. Constructing varying and often competing disability discourses around genetics, experience and policy may be academically expedient for some but, we believe, such practices are unlikely to change the materiality of this disturbing and deplorable situation.

We have chosen, therefore, the concepts of exclusion and inclusion as the central focus around which to organise this book. This is because:

Exclusion and inclusion are universal features of social interaction, and institutions serve to structure these processes, through states, markets, communities and voluntary associations.

(Jordan 1996: 39)

This choice is both fashionable and unfashionable at the same time: fashionable, in that this pair of concepts has been used to discuss and explain the economic and social marginalisation of a whole range of groups throughout the world; unfashionable because speaking in dualisms, it is often argued, is too simplistic a device to describe and examine the multiple realities of the postmodern world.

That be as it may, throughout history disabled people have experienced both exclusion and inclusion depending on a combination of economic, social, political, ideological, moral and cultural forces. In this book we attempt to deal with all of these rather than to focus merely on the cultural and the ideological as others have begun to do. It is divided into two distinct but related parts. Part One contains eight chapters outlining the central tenets of our argument. Part Two includes selected extracts from published documents pertinent to the issues raised.

The first chapter sets the scene and looks at the key issues facing British welfare if it is to become more inclusionary than it has been up to now in respect of disabled people. We point to the contradictions and dilemmas of state-provided welfare and suggest that an inclusionary vision tied to effective welfare practice can rescue the welfare state from its current difficulties as well as improving the lives of disabled people.

Chapter 2 poses the question: Who are disabled people? and suggests that the answers we have would be more useful for social policy if disabled people had not been excluded from the process of definition. We will look at recent attempts to define, describe and classify the population of disabled people. To do so we examine definitions provided by the World Health Organisation (WHO), the Union of the Physically Impaired Against Segregation (UPIAS), and Disabled People's International (DPI). We also critically evaluate the most recent and comprehensive work on disability undertaken by the Office of Population Censuses and Surveys (OPCS), renamed the Office for National Statistics on 1 April 1996. We suggest that attempts to define and classify who is and who is not disabled, as well as the degree of severity, are culturally determined. We also contend that recent developments led by the disabled people's movement have definite and positive implications for the creation of an inclusionary society.

Chapter 3 examines disability in history and culture. Based on what limited anthropological evidence is currently available, it begins with a broad overview of the ways in which disabled people have been excluded from and included in different societies throughout the world. We suggest that within the British context, exclusion has been far more common than inclusion, and that the reasons for this stemmed originally from ignorance and superstition and, more recently, from industrial development and its accompanying ideologies: scientific rationality, individualism and medicalisation. Although this may not appear to have any direct relevance to current social policy and welfare, we suggest that its ideological legacy informs both current policies and practices.

These themes are taken up in Chapter 4. Here we look at the development of social policy for disabled people in the post-1945 period. We argue that initially social policy either ignored disabled people or specifically sought to exclude them from mainstream British society through the development of separate facilities. We go on to argue that, in the main, late-twentieth century social policy, legislation and services, both in Britain and overseas, have tended to exclude, disempower and immiserate disabled people rather than include and empower them. This is mainly due to the fact that these programmes were based on a general misunderstanding of the real nature of disability and because disabled people were excluded from any meaningful role in the processes of policy development and service delivery.

Theories of disability and their implications for social policy are examined in Chapter 5. We show that the exclusion of disabled people from the generation and development of such theories has allowed traditional individualised medical approaches to disability based upon: personal tragedy theory, not just to define the realities of the experiences of impairment, but also to structure the development of political and policy responses to disabled people. The end result is the bewildering array of welfare institutions and services which continue to compound rather than alleviate the experience of both impairment and disability discussed in Chapter 4. Also included in this chapter is an overview of the more recent sociopolitical analyses of disability; with particular emphasis on the 'materialist' or barriers approach to disability frequently referred to as the 'social model of disability'.

Chapter 6 explores issues of identity and action and the ways in which the 'social model' has impacted on the lives of disabled people. Building on the issues raised on Chapter 4 we begin with an exploration of the meaning of disability within contemporary cultural forms and its relevance to the construction of a conventional disabled or 'dependent' identity. We then turn to the ways in which our understandings of disability have recently been transformed as a consequence of the appearance and growth of the disabled people's movement. The role of self-help, social and political organisations will be considered as a principal aspect of this process. We demonstrate that collective action has been a key feature of the emergence of positive disabled identities and that, taken together, these developments are beginning to force crucial and important changes on to the policy and welfare agenda.

In Chapter 7 we extend this analysis further and look at the struggles of the disabled people's movement for 'independent living'. The discussion centres on early initiatives such as the campaign for a comprehensive disability income, adequate and accessible disability information, integrated community-based housing schemes, centres for independent/

integrated living, personal assistance schemes, and the on-going battle for comprehensive and enforceable civil rights legislation. This discussion is located in the context of recent 'community care' initiatives and critically evaluates changing provision and practice. We argue that there is an urgent need for a meaningful and workable bottom-up approach to community-based support services based on the full inclusion of disabled people in all aspects of planning, provision and delivery.

The final chapter explores the potential of social policy and state welfare for transformation, emancipation and the coming of inclusive citizenship. We consider the changing political and social institutions of societies in the late-twentieth century and contemplate the possibilities for the empowerment of disabled people into the twenty-first century. Finally we argue that modern societies without welfare states at their heart will indeed be heartless societies, not just for disabled people but for everyone.

Part Two is divided into three distinct areas:

1. policy statements and documents produced by disabled people and their organisations
2. various international charters and documents emphasising the rights of disabled people
3. selected extracts from legislation and policy statements produced by successive British governments outlining the philosophy underpinning disability policy in the UK.

We have deliberately placed the documents in this order. Those emanating from disabled people have been placed first because we believe that they are not only the most important but also the most visionary. Second come documents from international charters which also contain visions of how the world ought to be. We then present extracts from official documents which attempt to deal with the world as it is. Finally we provide a list of relevant statutes and reports.

PART ONE

From exclusion to inclusion?

CHAPTER 1

The times are changing for the welfare state

Introduction

We are writing a book which is primarily about British social policy in respect of disabled people. However, we have to remember that we cannot merely bracket off the broader economic and social changes that are occurring throughout the world and affecting the lives of every single person on the planet.

> The recent convulsive changes in the organisation of capitalism – its global reach, its revolutionary technological innovations, its centralisation in giant corporations and financial institutions – have resulted in the virtual exclusion of vast numbers of the world's poor from effective economic and political participation.
>
> (Friedmann 1992: 14)

The concepts of exclusion and inclusion are central to our analysis and we analyse the origins, development and future of British welfare within this conceptual framework. In order to do so, in this chapter we spell out our own approach with regard to welfare and disability, focusing on the ways in which British welfare policy may both include and exclude disabled people from the mainstream of economic and social participation.

Setting the scene

In the past 20 years our understanding of disability has changed radically. We have gone from viewing 'disability' as a tragic problem occurring for isolated, unfortunate individuals for whom the only appropriate social response was medical treatment, to seeing it as a situation of collective institutional discrimination (Barnes 1991) and social oppression (Abberley 1987) to which the only appropriate response is political action (Oliver 1990; Campbell and Oliver 1996). Somewhere in between sits the welfare state, based neither wholly on personal tragedy theory nor fully embracing social oppression theory.

The construction of disability as a social problem neatly mirrored the emergence of the 'classic' welfare state as the creation of modernity. In the broadest sense, the term modernity denotes the complex process of industrial, political and cultural development following the appearance and rise of capitalism beginning at the turn of the eighteenth century.

Indeed, state involvevemnt in disabled people's lives has increased steadily throughout this period but the modern or classic welfare state emerged in the post-1945 period. However, this construction was based on 'liberal, humanistic individualism' (Leonard 1997) which, while recognising the need for collective social programmes, was underpinned by the individualistic medical model of disability derived from personal tragedy theory itself (Oliver 1996). Unfortunately, the classic welfare state never managed to resolve this contradiction providing therapeutic solutions to the problems of 'unfortunate' individuals rather than political action for excluded groups.

It would be easy to dismiss the classic welfare state as nothing more than a creation of modernity based on particular certainties of the period such as full employment, the nuclear family, the perfectibility of human beings through medicine and technology, and inclusive citizenship. The absence of exclusionary forces such as racism, sexism, disablism, ageism, homophobia and so on was widely ignored until excluded groups forced their exclusion first on to political and then on to welfare agendas.

The political consensus which sustained the classic welfare state began to break down at the same time as social theorists were lamenting or celebrating, depending on their point of view, the decline of modernity and the emergence of postmodernity. Into this hotchpotch of theoretical debate and political dispute, the classic welfare state has been pitched and tossed to the point where it is becoming unrecognisable in the same way that postmodernity is being seen as fundamentally different from the modernity which it is purported to have replaced.

The problems with the postmodernist worldview are well known though often not spoken about. Its ahistoricity tends to ignore the past which means that important lessons are not learned. Its recipes for political action are often divisive and sectional and, when linked to social policy and welfare issues, can sound like special pleading. Its analysis of the exclusionary processes of postmodernity are limited to cultural analyses of difference and lack any committed vision of what could be and indeed what ought to be, save that difference be celebrated and exclusion ended despite the fact that 'the value of diversity is insufficient to provide a basis for an emancipatory struggle' (Leonard 1997: 29).

We are not convinced that modernity can be dismissed or that postmodernity should be embraced in the ways that are currently fashionable. We do not see where we are now as somewhere different from where we were 50 or 20 years ago: rather, we are confronted with the same issues that we have always been confronted with, even if the circumstances in which we confront them have changed and are changing. For us capitalism continues to rule OK! even if it is now global rather than based on the nation state.

The classic welfare state as an attempt to humanise capitalism has produced both benefits and problems, it has included and excluded. The changing welfare state will, and should, continue to attempt to humanise changing capitalism. In so doing, it will remain on the horns of the contradictions of capitalism; it will exclude as well as include, it will control as well as care, it will promise rights yet endorse charity, it will promote independence but produce dependence, it will empower and it will disempower.

Postmodernist theorising will dismiss this preliminary analysis of the welfare state as being locked into a modernist way of thinking which inevitably produces dualisms. Nevertheless, like Clause Offe, we believe that 'capitalism cannot coexist with, neither can it exist without, the welfare state' (Offe 1984: 153). We maintain that failure to see the potential as well as the dangers of collective welfare provision will inevitably mean that the lessons of history will be ignored and that dominant welfare discourses will continue to be dominated by the rhetoric and policies of the powerful.

Our own approach

Our approach to collective welfare provision for disabled people is rooted in disabled people's own analysis of why we are excluded and oppressed, and the collective solutions we have arrived at after many years of struggle with welfare institutions and the policy makers, professionals and managers who dominate them. It is for this reason that Part Two of this book contains a series of documents on these themes produced by disabled people themselves.

The fact that our analysis is rooted in disabled people's own collective worldview does not mean that we are against theory and the academics who develop it. Our argument, more fully explored elsewhere (Oliver 1996: Chapter 10), is that academics as 'organic intellectuals' have a key role to play in the development of our knowledge about the world in which we live. The term 'organic intellectuals' is rooted in the work of the Italian Marxist and political activist Antonio Gramsci and his discussion of working-class movements where the development and control of ideas are often the outcome of the intervention of 'middle-class' theorists (Gramsci 1971). Hence, 'positional' or 'situational' intellectuals are those who locate themselves within a particular situation in order to write about it. 'Organic' intellectuals, on the other hand, are those who write about social issues based on direct personal experience. Indeed, our role is that of interpreting emerging collective experience rather than imposing our own views on it.

At this point it is worth summarising our position on the issues we discuss in this book.

- we do not see the current situation as postmodernity having replaced modernity, nor the welfare state as the epitome of humane modernity, now outmoded
- we see the late-twentieth century as part of the continuing development of capitalism, and for this reason we prefer, and subsequently use, the term late capitalism rather than postmodernity
- we see the changing welfare state as a continuing contradiction of late capitalism

• we see ourselves as activists struggling with other disabled people to ameliorate and eventually eliminate these contradictions and this work as part of that struggle at the intellectual level.

In the rest of this chapter we examine some of the contradictions that the late capitalist welfare state imposes for disabled people. The list is not intended to be exhaustive.

Now and then

What we have called the classic welfare state was built on the premise of full employment as a central policy objective. Moreover, legislation was initially enacted to ensure that disabled people secured their fair share of this employment (see Document (L) in Part Two). However, good intentions are no guarantee of outcomes and disabled people have never managed to secure their fair share of the available employment because of a combination of inflexible working practices, unregulated labour markets and prejudice and discrimination from employers and unions alike (Barnes 1991).

The welfare state sought to resolve this problem but effectively colluded with the forces which were excluding disabled people from the world of work. It did this by failing to enforce disabled peoples' rights under the law and instead concentrated on providing employment rehabilitation programmes and technical support for disabled individuals seeking work. The contradiction in this policy was that while it enabled a small number of disabled individuals to compete in the world of work as it was, it effectively excluded the vast majority of disabled people capable of working (Barnes 1991; Thornton and Lunt 1995; Hyde 1996).

Struggling to live

Another central plank of the classic welfare state was intended to provide support for living and while different kinds of institutions were targeted for closure at different times, it was based on the premise that people should live in their own homes and not institutions. As far as disabled people are concerned, this premise was never fully embraced and a variety of institutions including Cheshire homes, local authority part 3 accommodation and young chronic sick units, known as Young Disabled Units (YDUs) were created. While these institutions never warehoused more than a minority of disabled people, they attracted the lion's share of the support for living funding to the point that many disabled people felt that their only choice was to survive without support or go into an institution.

The contradiction that this created was that while the welfare state was supposed to enable disabled people to live independently, the vast majority were forced into dependency. This meant many disabled individuals survived only with the help of relatives and friends. For those whose families were unwilling or unable to cope, or who were determined not to accept such dependency, the institution was usually the only solution. It is for this reason that the Union of the Physically Impaired Against Segregation (UPIAS) focused its critique of state welfare on the institution, and saw its abolition as a central plank of the emerging disabled peoples' movement (see Document (A) in Part Two).

The ideological dominance that the institution continues to exert over the lives of disabled people can best be understood in the same way as the ideological hegemony that the workhouse exerted over nineteenth-century paupers. Disabled people still live in fear that if their support arrangements break down, their financial situation changes or the state changes its rules, they will be forced into the twentieth-century equivalent of the nineteenth-century workhouse. So the contradiction of the classic welfare state continues into the changing welfare state of late capitalism: while independence is encouraged and promoted, the institution remains the enforcement mechanism for this.

Health for all?

Health care for all, free at the point of delivery, was another central plank of the classic welfare state. Supported by medical and technological advances, initial optimism was that the problems associated with ill health would be abolished, by abolishing the disease on which it was based. The problem for many disabled people was that their impairments, even if they were disease-based, were not amenable to being cured by medical advances. This in itself created problems for rehabilitation as it was and it remains based on the assumption that disabled individuals can be restored to 'normal functioning' where cure was unavailable.

The ideology of the cure was also powerful because of the fact that it is founded on and perpetuates notions of the perfectibility of human beings. Those not able to conform to perfectibility criteria were seen as inferior and in need of regulation and control. 'Personal tragedy theory' fed into this ideology to the point where disabled people were never asked whether or not they wanted to be cured; and the idea of eradicating disabled people from society was, and continues to be, promoted as a worthy social goal.

The contradiction that this exposes is that of trying to ensure that some of the very real benefits of medical and technological advances are not allowed to run unchecked and raise the spectre of genocide once again. The continued exclusion of disabled people from these debates makes the possibility of such a spectre becoming a reality more rather than less likely. Already we could eradicate a whole range of conditions and, with the number increasing continually, a proper debate about the implications of this is long overdue.

The slow and the fast

The idea of inclusive education for all children was another key plank of the classic welfare state and this included disabled children (see Document (K) in Part Two). Unfortunately, however, the philosophy underpinning the initial legislation was not properly translated into inclusive educational provision and practice. A combination of the commitment to meet the individual educational needs of each disabled child coupled with the dominance of the traditional individualistic medical model of disability within the educational establishment served to ensure the establishment and an infrastructure of special segregated provision.

While the late capitalist welfare state has modified this to some extent (Norwich 1997), large numbers of disabled children continue to be educated in isolation from their non-disabled peers. While there is universal agreement that disabled people should be fully integrated into society, the contradiction that segregated schooling imposes is that it sees exclusion in early life as the most appropriate mechanism for ensuring this ultimate inclusion. However, there is no evidence that this marginally modified policy has succeeded in ensuring inclusion and the negative effects of preventing disabled children from being educated alongside their peers are now being realised.

Sink or swim

The classic welfare state was premised on the nuclear family which would provide the vast majority of support for individuals with little or no support from the state. In reality this meant that, by and large, women were expected to shoulder the burden of domestic labour, unsupported and unwaged. This included providing disabled people with the assistance they needed where they were not placed in an institution.

This enforced reliance on family members has posed dilemmas for disabled people and other family members and has resulted in what we can only describe as a moral panic about carers. The term itself is ideological dynamite as it serves to position disabled people as non-caring and dependent and those family members who provide necessary support as caring and committed (Keith and Morris 1996). This is, of course, both a gross oversimplification of the reality of family life as well as being oppressive to disabled people.

The discovery of the 'carer' in the late capitalist welfare state has sharpened the contradictions imposed by the approach to families of state welfare policies. Constructing the category carer and developing policies in respect of this group has neither enabled disabled people to become independent nor freed other family members from their 'caring' duties. In fact, apart from inventing a new word and giving employment to yet more welfare professionals and opportunist voluntary organisations, nothing much has changed and the contradictions of family life remain.

Who gets what?

The classic welfare state established the principle that all those who needed them should be provided with a range of community based services. As far as disabled people were concerned, while the initial list (National Assistance Act 1948) was short, it was expanded considerably at a later stage (Chronically Sick and Disabled Persons Act 1970) (see Document (N) in Part Two). The problem, however, was that the services listed were discretionary, were rigidly controlled by professionals in their role as gatekeepers and often simply not provided at all.

Under the traditional welfare state, local authorities could only provide services or contract them to other providers; the provision of cash rather than services was illegal, even if a few imaginative authorities, in combination with disabled people and emergent user-led organisations, began to ignore the law. Moreover, the widespread dissatisfaction with provider-led, professionally dominated provision within the disabled population led directly to increasingly vociferous demands from disabled people and their organisations for meaningful control of the services on which they were forced to depend.

These demands coincided with the marketisation of welfare, characteristic of the welfare state emerging in late capitalism, and provides a further contradiction between collective welfare based on services and individualised welfare based on the market. Disabled people and their organisations have already gone some way to resolving this contradiction locally by setting up various support groups (collective) to ensure that their forays into the market are based on sound consumer advice (individual).

Losers and winners

The welfare state is neither one thing nor another; it is a contradiction. Thus, if seven out of ten disabled people are excluded from the workforce, three out of ten are included; if nine out of ten disabled children are educated into dependency, one in ten go on to higher education or work rather than segregation in the day centre, further education unit, or within their family; if the majority of disabled people and their families are forced to accept professionally dominated, dependency creating state services, a few manage to establish and control their own independent living packages.

We do not take the view that, by allowing a few people to succeed and be included, this serves to legitimate the whole system. Wolfensberger (1989), for example, argues that the welfare state (or human services as he calls them) are deliberately designed to foster dependency in order to give employment to the middle classes. He goes on to suggest that

> there are always a few people somewhere who get habilitated into greater independence and competence, thus serving as a cover or front for the service supersystem.
>
> (Wolfensberger 1989: 34)

This success, for the vast majority of disabled people who have succeeded, has not been bestowed on them but has emerged out of the struggles for inclusion and the sustained and penetrating critiques of state welfare that have been an essential part of those struggles. Failure to recognise this will inevitably mean failure to learn from the lessons of our history and to realise that it is possible to create enabling and inclusive welfare structures, as disabled people have already begun to do. The trick, if that is what it is, is to include disabled people at all stages in the planning, delivery and control of these services.

Will the welfare state survive?

The inadequacies of the classic welfare state and the dangers of the marketised welfare state of late capitalism, have been one of a number of key factors around which disabled people have begun to collectively organise themselves (Campbell and Oliver 1996). This collective empowerment has been seen as a powerful threat to entrenched professional attitudes and practices and the vested interests of the traditional voluntary sector who have a lot to lose when disabled people begin to speak for themselves rather than rely on non-representative others to speak for them.

Both state services and the voluntary sector have opportunistically responded to the challenge posed by disabled people's self-organisation by embracing the concept of empowerment to the point where there are numerous texts advising on how to empower (Stevenson and Parsloe 1993; James 1994) and conferences where the powerful talk endlessly about how to empower the disempowered. The contradiction in all this is that empowerment is only something people can do for themselves because, ultimately, deciding to empower someone else, whether they want it or not, is the most disempowering thing that can be done to them.

This has led some disabled people, notably Vic Finkelstein and Ossie Stuart (1996), to conclude that the only way to eradicate 'the welfare mentality rooted in a disabling culture' is to remove services from health and welfare departments and place support in the hands of departments responsible for the environment in its broadest sense. While this radical solution has some merit, it would further disadvantage many disabled people in terms of their access to heath care and social support, as well as fundamentally denying the role of collective welfare in creating the inclusive society. Furthermore, it raises the obvious question: are those currently in control at relevant government departments such as the Department of the Environment, for example, any more likely to give up their power than those at the Department of Health?

Welfare state, welfare society

The final contradiction has revolved around the issues of inclusion and exclusion itself. The welfare state, whether in its classic or late capitalist mode, is supposed to ensure the inclusion of all into the fabric of society and while the consensus about how to ensure inclusion may have broken down, its ultimate aim remains central to state-provided welfare. However, as we go on to demonstrate in the case of disabled people, often welfare programmes can either exclude themselves, as in the case of segregated provision such as residential homes, day centres and special schools, or collude with other exclusionary forces as in the case of family policies and the failure to provide ethnically sensitive services (Barnes 1991).

The contradictions of the welfare state do not mean that it is nothing more than an ideological trick as some Marxist analyses have implied, or that it is a worthy but failed modernist project as some postmodernist analyses suggest. Moreover, we do not agree with new right thinking which suggests that collective welfare is both too costly and inefficient as well as bound to encourage dependency on the state (George and Wilding 1994).

While we do not deny the force of the critiques that these analyses pose, we see the welfare state as offering the same opportunities that it has always offered: those for inclusion rather than exclusion. While we need, through sustained and constructive critique, to deconstruct the practices of state welfare in order to decide which are exclusionary and which not, we also need to ensure that reconstruction takes place. This reconstruction is not merely an intellectual process engaged in future imaginings, but a programme of action built on the experience of struggle out of which will inevitably emerge a truly inclusionary welfare state.

Indeed, in respect of disabled people, not only has the critique of state welfare already had a significant influence on provision and practice, but also that action borne out of the experience of struggle has began to put in place the building blocks for truly inclusionary forms of welfare.

> To be excluded from the upper echelons of power is not necessarily to be condemned to a life without history . . . The struggle for survival can take many forms. Some are acts of individual enterprise in the informal economy; some are collective acts of protest and defiance; still others are centred in the community. All initiatives require the co-operation of others; most require some form of outside help from students, priests and professionals who may provide the catalytic spark in the face of adversity.
>
> (Friedmann 1992: 22)

Conclusion

This chapter has provided the framework on which we interrogate the development of social policy in respect of disabled people, examine its current practices and suggest approaches for its future. Just as one cultural icon of the twentieth century, Bob Dylan, has concluded that the times in general are a'changing, so too one eminent sociological icon, Anthony Giddens, suggests that the times for the welfare state are also changing:

The class compromise of welfare institutions could remain relatively stable only so long as the conditions of simple modernization held good. These were circumstances in which industriousness and paid work remained central to the social system: where class relations were closely linked to communal forms; where the nation-state was strong and even in some respects further developing its sovereign powers; and where risk could still be treated largely as external and to be coped with by quite orthodox programmes of social insurance. None of these conditions holds in the same way in conditions of intensifying globalisation and social reflexivity.

(Giddens 1994: 149)

CHAPTER 2

Who are disabled people?

Introduction

Head-counting, or number-crunching as it is sometimes called, has long been regarded as an essential element of social policy because, so it is argued, governments are unlikely to commit resources to particular policy initiatives unless they can be reasonably sure of the numbers of people who may benefit and have some idea of the costs involved. We are not convinced of this and argue that in respect of disability policy, such attempts have failed because, essentially, they have focused on the wrong thing; that is they have tried to measure the numbers of disabled people rather than the effects of disabling environments.

A major factor in this has been the wholesale exclusion of disabled people from the policy-making process almost since the inception of the idea that governments must make policy responses to the problems of disabled people. Although, hitherto, this particular form of exclusion has been almost total, increasingly in the last 20 years disabled people have begun to insist that our voices should be included in all aspects of policy debate, including debates about how we should be defined and classified.

Accordingly we look at recent attempts to define, describe and classify the population of disabled people throughout the world, looking at definitions provided by the World Health Organisation (WHO), the Union of the Physically Impaired Against Segregation (UPIAS) and Disabled Peoples International (DPI). We also critically examine recent work on disability undertaken by the Office of Population Censuses and Surveys (OPCS) in Britain, now known as the Office for National Statistics. Finally, we suggest that at international, national and local levels we must move away from sterile exercises in head-counting and number-crunching and instead focus on classifying disabling environments and measuring disabling barriers, for only then will we be able to develop relevant and appropriate policy initiatives.

Definitions and terminology

The first task here is to clarify the terminology used throughout this book. This is important because language is central not just to the ways we define and classify particular groups but also to our understanding of the world. We use words to ascribe meaning to situations and objects and orient our behaviour accordingly. Moreover, definitions of disability are frequently vague, malleable and used interchangeably. Consequently, it is often difficult to understand what is meant by policy-makers, researchers, the lay public, and sometimes disabled people themselves in discussions on this particular issue.

In Western culture, there are at least two reasons for this situation. Historically, 'disability' has always been an important category in the crucial division between the 'deserving' and the 'undeserving' poor; those defined as unable as opposed to those unwilling to work (Stone 1985). Throughout the twentieth century the process of categorisation has become ever more sophisticated with the involvement of a seemingly never ending list of professional 'experts'. These include doctors, lawyers, benefit administrators, policy analysts, therapists and researchers, each of whom have their own interpretation of the concept and its use according to their own particular interests and criteria. All these people and others are involved in what Gary Albrecht (1992) has referred to as the 'disability business'.

The second reason why definitions are important arises from what might be termed the politics of language. Since at least the 1950s there has been a growing realisation that our understanding of hitherto controversial social issues such as disability can be transformed through the use of language. Several disadvantaged groups including women, minority ethnic groups, lesbians and gay men have challenged traditional social constructions and stereotypes by identifying the sexist, racist and heterosexist biases underpinning established definitions and terminology. For example, terms such as 'man' when used generically in isolation in discussions of human development undermine the role of women in society.

Similarly, the disabled people's movement has realised that definitions and terminology play a significant role in their individual and collective disadvantage. Terms such as 'cripple', 'spastic' and 'mongol' are offensive when used to refer to a disabled individual. Others which depersonalise and objectify the disabled community are also considered unacceptable. Examples include 'the disabled', 'the deaf' or 'the blind'. Further, in an effort to overturn traditional negative assumptions and attitudes surrounding disability, organisations controlled and run by disabled people have developed definitions and terminology of their own (Barnes 1992; Campbell and Oliver 1996).

As a result, although there are a number of variations, definitions of disability can be divided into two distinct groups: official definitions produced by professionals and academics, and those developed by disabled people and organisations controlled and run by them.

Official definitions

In an effort to provide consistency and minimise confusions over definitions and terminology, the World Health Organisations (WHO) commissioned Doctor Philip Wood at Manchester University to expand on the existing 'International Classification of Disease' to cover the consequences of long-term illness. The result 'The International Classification of Impairment, Disability and Handicap' (ICIDH) was published in 1980. Widely regarded as the most comprehensive catalogue of its kind, it has been used as a basis for government initiatives on disability in both the well-resourced, minority world of Europe and North America, and the majority world of poorly resourced, 'developing' nations of the south and east.

Drawing heavily on previous work by the British government's Office of Populations, Censuses and Surveys (OPCS) (Harris 1971), the ICIDH uses a three-fold typology of 'impairment', 'disability' and 'handicap'. Thus, an impairment refers to 'any loss or abnormality of psychological, physiological or anatomical structure or function'. 'Disability' denotes 'any restriction or lack (resulting from an impairment) of ability to perform an activity in the manner or within the range considered normal for a human being'. 'Handicap' is defined as 'a disadvantage for a given individual, resulting from an impairment or disability, that limits or prevents the fulfilment of a role that is normal (depending on age, sex and social and cultural factors) for that individual' (Wood 1980: 29).

Clearly, this typology is founded on assumptions about the existence and nature of intellectual and physical 'normality'. Disability and handicap are caused by psychological or physiological 'abnormality' or impairment and, therefore, the impairment is the primary focus of attention. There are a number of problems with this approach.

First, psychological and physical normality are not easily defined, nor are their corresponding impairments. Indeed, all definitions of social phenomena (which normality and impairment are) are dependent on temporal, cultural and situational factors. For present purposes Leonard Davis (1995) suggests that the word 'normal' only enters the English language around 1840. It is surely no coincidence that this is the same time that the pressures of industrialisation were forcing governments to define, classify and control populations (see Chapter 4).

Second, implicit in the ICIDH is the assertion that the human being is flexible and adaptable while the physical and/or social environments are not. This clearly flies in the face of reality since historically humans have always moulded the environment to suit their needs rather than the other way round.

Third, since psychological or physiological impairments are presented as the cause of disability and handicap, it follows that they should be 'cured' by psychological or medical intervention. People with impairments become objects to be treated, changed, improved and made 'normal'. While medical intervention to treat illness and disease may be quite appropriate, it is increasingly argued by a growing number of disabled people that it is quite inappropriate to treat disability (Oliver 1990, 1996; Barnes 1991; Morris 1991). As the disabled writer and poet, Simon Brisenden, observed:

In the past, especially, doctors have been too willing to suggest medical treatment and hospitalization, even when this would not necessarily improve the quality of life for the person concerned. Indeed, questions about the quality of life have sometimes been portrayed as an intrusion upon the medical equation.

(Brisenden 1986: 176)

Fourth, these definitions suggest that impairment, disability and handicap are essentially static states. Apart from the fact that this is inaccurate, it creates artificial distinctions and barriers between people with and without impairments where there need not be any (Sutherland 1981; Zola 1981). Such a situation is particularly ludicrous considering the range of conditions included in the ICIDH schema. In terms of impairment, besides a whole host of illnesses and diseases, conditions such as 'baldness', 'pregnancy' and 'homosexuality' are listed. With reference to 'disability', categories such as 'failure to get to work on time' or 'lack of interest in local or world events' are included; conditions which might easily be questions of choice or environment rather than of organic or intellectual pathology. As the disabled writer Tom Shakespeare (1994: 104) has observed, the ICIDH: 'has a classification for every feature of human physicality'.

Fifth, besides reflecting a particularly narrow set of Eurocentric values – namely, those of predominantly male, healthy, middle-class professionals – the ICIDH has provided neither consistency nor clarity. For example, in addition to the above the ICIDH defines handicap as 'a discordance between the individual's performance or status and the expectations of the group of which he [*sic*] is a member'; the same could be said of both 'impairment' and 'disability', making consistency of usage very difficult.

Finally, it has been argued by disabled activists that many of these problems have arisen because much of the work done on definitions has been carried out by people who do not themselves experience the daily problems of living with disability (Davis 1986). This is not an argument against research *per se* but one against research which seeks to be scientific and objective by excluding the real experience of disability from the research process.

Indeed, the ICIDH has not been very successful as a tool for classifying disabled people and there have been very few studies which have managed to operationalise it properly. Even the United Nations (UN) in its recent study (Despouy 1993) failed to make use of it. As a consequence the WHO is currently seeking to revise the whole scheme and to add a fourth, environmental dimension, more of which will be said later in this chapter.

Disabled peoples movement's definitions

The first definition produced by an organisation exclusive to people who do experience disability daily is the one developed in Britain by the Union of the Physically Impaired Against Segregation (UPIAS) in 1975.

In contrast to the already established OPCS definition, the UPIAS produced a two-tier classification. As with the OPCS and WHO schemes, the term impairment focuses on the body defining the term as 'lacking all or part of a limb, or having a defective limb, organism or mechanism of the body'. But disability denotes:

the disadvantage or restriction caused by a contemporary social organisation which takes no or little account of people who have physical impairments and thus excludes them from the mainstream of social activities.

(UPIAS 1976: 14)

The principle difference between this and previous definitions concern causality (Oliver 1996). As we have seen, the OPCS, and later the WHO, definitions are both reducible to individual and biological pathology; in contrast, the UPIAS version locates the causes of disability squarely on society and social organisation. In 1982, this two-fold definition was adopted and adapted by Disabled People's International (DPI) (Dreidger 1989) – the international umbrella for organisations controlled and run by disabled people – as follows. Disability denotes: 'the functional limitation within the individual caused by physical, sensory or mental impairments' and handicap is the: 'loss or limitation of opportunities to take part in the normal life of the community on an equal level with others due to physical and social barriers' (DPI 1982: 105).

There are at least three important differences between this and the UPIAS definition. First, the terms 'disability' and 'handicap' have been substituted for the words impairment and disability. This was considered necessary at the time, 1981, because it was felt that the words 'disability' and 'handicap' had a much wider currency at the international level, notably, in America and Canada. Second, the first element of the typology has been expanded to accommodate people with intellectual and sensory impairments.

Although still in use there are a number of problems with the terminology used by DPI. First and foremost the use of the term 'handicap' is offensive to many disabled people in both America (Albrecht 1992) and in the UK (Barnes 1992) largely because of its historical allusions to 'cap in hand', charity and begging. The word 'mental' is also considered oppressive by people with psychological impairments (Beresford and Wallcraft 1997). Consequently, elements within DPI have recently adopted UPIAS's original terminology and the word intellectual has replaced the term 'mental' (DPI 1994). This is in line with the terminology used by the British Council of Organisations of Disabled People (BCODP) – Britain's umbrella for organisations controlled and run by disabled people themselves – since its inception in 1981.

Finally, a further problem with the DPI definition concerns the use of the term 'normal'. The question of normality is a highly contentious issue; what is 'normal' for one section of the community may be 'abnormal' for another. Moreover, because historically the notion of normality has been widely used as a justification for the oppression of disabled people and, indeed, other minority groups, increasingly, disability theorists working from within a sociopolitical perspective opt for the wording of the UPIAS definition but without the inclusion of the word 'physical'. Thus, disability refers to: 'the disadvantage or restriction caused by a contemporary social organisation which takes no or little account of people who have . . . impairments and thus excludes them from the mainstream of social activities'. This means that use of the phrase 'people with disabilities' is unacceptable because it blurs the crucial distinction between impairment and disability. Additionally, though the tendency to place the noun 'people' before 'disability' is viewed positively by some, because it is intended to emphasise the fact that individuals with impairments are in fact people – something which, as we shall see later, has historically been denied – it has a number of important negative implications which need to be explored.

'People with disabilities' also implies that disability is the property of the individual and not of society. Here the terms 'disabilities' and 'disability' refer to a medical condition; since the 1970s disabled people and their organisations have rejected the implications of the medical model of disability. Further, by linking 'disability' to 'impairment', this phrase conveniently sidesteps the social and environmental barriers encountered by disabled people and, by implication, the need for change. Finally, it is an explicit denial of a political or 'disabled identity'. Since the emergence of the disabled people's movement, particularly in Britain, the word 'disabled' before 'people' or 'person' has come to signify identification with this collective identity. Phrases such as 'people with disabilities' tend to undermine that identity (Barnes 1992).

However, for the purposes of this book 'impairment' will refer to the medical condition, and 'disability' will be used as a generic term to refer to externally imposed disadvantage and social restriction. The vexed question of causality is not at issue here but will be dealt with later. In the interests of both clarity and those outlined immediately above we shall use the phrase 'disabled people' as opposed to 'people with disabilities'.

The point to emphasise is that there has been a long-running conflict between official and disabled peoples' own definitions, leading to the following call at a recent European conference of disabled people:

this meeting on human rights expresses its non support for the current classification of impairment, disability and handicap operated by the World Health Organisation. We call upon the WHO to enter into a dialogue with disabled people's organisations to adopt a new definition in line with the above resolution.

(DPI 1994, unpaged)

Partly as a consequence of this, and partly, as we go on to describe, because the WHO scheme has not proved very useful to policy-makers and politicians, the WHO is currently attempting to amend it, and is proposing to add a fourth, environmental dimension. While the involvement of disabled people in this process is better than before, many of us believe that the scheme remains fundamentally flawed and should be scrapped.

We hope that the discussion so far has helped to demonstrate that the issue of language is not merely an exercise in semantics and an attempt to force 'political correctness' on an unaccepting world but instead an attempt to inject an important and meaningful voice into an exclusionary process. We now go on to suggest that because of this exclusion and despite the resources expended, the information we have about disability is neither very accurate nor very useful and that including disabled peoples' views is likely to produce information of more relevance to the policy-making process.

The demography of disability

Given the problem of definition outlined above it goes without saying that any attempt to quantify the numbers of disabled people must be treated with the utmost caution, especially if we use the ICIDH as a basis for analysis. The use of statistics is a constant source of debate within sociology and social policy.

Since the work of nineteenth-century sociologists such as Emile Durkheim and Max Weber, the idea of a value free 'science of society' has had a powerful influence on twentieth-century sociologists and social policy analysts, especially in America. In fact Durkheim's study of suicide (Lukes 1973) using national statistics as it did, has been cited as both an exemplar of how to do social research as well as an exemplar of how not to do it. The main critical argument is that the use of statistics is merely a reflection of a particular view of the world which tends to obscure other important theoretical and qualitative issues.

These problems are intensified when dealing with official statistics produced by governments and the state. This is because despite their claim to objectivity and neutrality, official statistics play a crucial role in the reproduction of ideology and culture (Miles and Irvine 1979) and they need to be interpreted with caution (Levitas and Guy 1996).

There is a well-established tradition of empirical investigations of the disabled population involving policy-makers, planners, academics and researchers. In Britain, for example, there have been several attempts to gather statistics about disabled people, beginning with the census of 1851 which asked questions about visual and hearing impairments. But these were dropped in 1921 because it was considered too difficult to phrase appropriate questions in such a general survey. In the post-Second World War period, however, legislation such as the Disabled Persons (Employment) Act 1944, and the Chronically Sick and Disabled Persons Act 1970, required local registers of disabled people to be kept. There have also been two attempts by the OPCS to quantify the disabled population at the national level.

The first OPCS survey was conducted in the 1960s to facilitate the expansion of services for disabled people as part of a general programme of increased welfare expenditure. The second was commissioned by the government in 1984 with the explicit aim of updating information about disability in Britain not including Northern Ireland. The first study estimated that there were 3 071 000 'handicapped' adults in the UK; the second produced a figure of 6.2 million: 14.2 per cent of the British population not including children.

The discrepancy between the two does not mean that the numbers of disabled people have doubled in the 15 years between the surveys but can be accounted for largely on methodological grounds. To begin with each survey used a different definition; the first focused entirely on physical 'handicaps' while the second, based as it was on the ICIDH, included sensory and intellectual impairments.

Additionally Peter Townsend (1979) has argued that this was due to the fact that the Harris Survey adopted too narrow a definition. He states:

disability itself might be best defined as inability to perform the activities, share in the relationships and play the roles which are customary for people of broadly the same age and sex in society.

(Townsend 1979: 691)

Using a much broader definition, Townsend himself estimated that there were 9 900 000 disabled people in the UK. However, it should be noted that he included children, while they were excluded from the Harris study.

The WHO definition formed the basis for the OPCS's second survey of disability during the 1980s (Martin *et al.* 1988). Again the focus was on 'functional ability' or as the OPCS researchers put it 'disability'. However, according to them, it is misleading to think of people as disabled or otherwise, as disability or functional limitations can only be considered in terms of a continuum. While this may be seen as something of a step forward from previous classification systems, it did not prevent the OPCS researchers from devising a ten-point severity scale denoting the extent of disability, nor a complex set of individualising and oppressive questions with which to decide who was and who was not disabled. Moreover, following interviews with only 2231 individuals, they calculated that there are 6.2 million disabled people in the UK. In a separate survey of children under 16 they estimated that there are 360 000 disabled children in Britain and they also included people with 'intellectual impairments'.

Much of the discrepancy between these three studies can, therefore, be accounted for in terms of the different definitions used; hence our earlier assertion that there is more at stake in attempting to define the world than merely choosing the right words. However, as Paul Abberley (1991, 1996) has pointed out, disability is a relative concept, not a static one, and is a function of the relationship between individual impairment and social situation. Therefore, any attempt to reduce this to counting individuals must ultimately be dependent on the definition used. To put it crudely, it would be possible to come up with a definition which meant that every one was disabled or, alternatively, one in which there were few if any disabled people.

Despite these problems, it is often argued that it is essential to policy development to have a reasonable idea of the numbers of people who will be involved – otherwise, so the argument goes, it is impossible to cost the proposals accurately. However, we argue that none of the studies discussed provide accurate estimates because there is no fixed number of disabled people; disability is dependent on the environments in which impaired people are placed.

For example, data from the Harris (1971) survey was used to estimate the numbers of disabled people likely to be eligible for a new benefit the then government wanted to introduce. This was to be called the Attendance Allowance and, extrapolating from the Harris survey, it was estimated that a maximum of 25 000 disabled people were likely to be eligible. Within the first year 75 000 people had qualified to receive the benefit despite the fact that stringent eligibility criteria were rigidly applied (Oliver 1983).

Similarly, following the Martin *et al.* (1988) survey, the government decided to establish the Independent Living Fund (ILF) to assist a small number of disabled people to employ personal assistants. It confidently allocated £5 million to the Fund for the first year, but within five years expenditure had risen to over £70 million and the government was so alarmed that it closed the ILF to potential new applicants (see Chapter 7).

These examples, along with the general critiques of positivist approaches to social policy (for example, Finch 1986), lead us to seriously doubt the value of head-counting and number-crunching, however sophisticatedly it is presented, as an aid to social policy formulation. Because of these doubts we have been accused (Bury 1996) of double standards in that while being roundly critical of such studies, we have nonetheless continued to quote their findings. While it is true that we have used the ball-park figures, we have always suggested that on pragmatic grounds, the studies simply do not, and indeed cannot, provide information sufficiently accurate to facilitate policy-making nor indeed to improve the material conditions under which disabled people live out their lives.

It is possible to focus on measuring 'disabling environments' instead of continuing to try to count the numbers of disabled individuals and, indeed, one such study has recently been undertaken by the influential Policy Studies Institute (Zarb 1995). The idea for this emerged from a joint conference organised by the BCODP and the Social Science Research Group and was published in a paper the following year (Oliver 1987).

The project has produced both quantitative and qualitative evidence of both the nature and extent of disabling barriers that disabled people face to feed into the policy-making process. Such information is likely to be much more useful than previous research in that it will provide an evidential basis for the development of policies designed to facilitate barrier removal. While the project has not been without its difficulties (Zarb 1997), it has sought to include disabled people in all aspects of the research process.

The problem with counting the numbers of disabled people is even more problematic at the international level. Until recently, it was thought that approximately 10 per cent of the world's population are disabled people. But recent research suggests that such a blanket figure is an overestimation which overlooks the wide variation of impairments and consequently disability within and between different countries. It may be more or less depending on a wide variety of factors: the age structure of populations, the level of technological and medical development, the extent of poverty, the presence or absence of war and the kind of economy are all involved in the production of impairment and the creation of disability. But as a general rule, the prevalence of both impairment and disability is higher in wealthier 'developed' countries than it is in poorer 'developing' ones, and there are more disabled people in urban areas than there are in rural communities.

For example, house-to-house surveys conducted in villages near Madras in India by PREPARE, a local organisation involved in community health programmes, found that only 1 per cent of the population were disabled people (Coleridge 1993). The United Nations (UN) Disability Statistics Compendium (1990) shows that Peru, Ethiopia, Pakistan and Sri Lanka have a disability rate of only 1 per cent. But Australia, Britain, Canada and Spain have 11 per cent and over. Austria has .the highest incidence of disability with a figure of 21 per cent.

Clearly, the figures appear to contradict the general view that there are more impaired people in developing countries where poverty and deprivation are common. There are a number of reasons for this. First, wealthy countries tend to have better health and support services; hence, there is a greater survival rate among people born with impairments and among those who acquire them later in life. Second, the demographic bias toward old age in most developed societies means that the prevalence of disability is higher among the general population; in all societies the likelihood of acquiring an impairment increases significantly with age. Third, conditions regarded as 'disabling' in highly developed industrialised societies, such as 'dyslexia' or 'flat feet', for example, would present few problems to someone living in a rural village in Zimbabwe (Coleridge 1993).

The figures also suggest that there is an urban bias towards impairment within all societies. This is because in urban areas there are generally more medical and 'rehabilitation' services, a greater risk of injury through road and/or industrial accident, a prevalence of sedentary occupations, and the possibility of earning a living by begging. It is not uncommon in cities in poor countries where begging is common for children to be maimed deliberately in order to make them more successful beggars. In some societies, racial factors are significant too. In South Africa, for example, important differences in the quality of medical services for different racial groups means that a spinally injured White person is ten times more likely to survive into late middle age than a Black contemporary (Coleridge 1993).

At the same time, there is considerable variation in rural areas. In certain villages in Zaire, for example, more than 30 per cent of the community are affected by river blindness. The recent upsurge of civil wars within a number of developing countries has also resulted in an unprecedented growth in the numbers of disabled people yet to be counted. In 1993 Peter Coleridge, for example, reported that Cambodia had many people with missing limbs because of the extensive use of landmines by the warring factions.

Similarly, in Angola the 'low intensity conflict' (LIC) conducted by UNITA forces in the late 1980s resulted in a significant growth in the disabled population. In this type of conflict, permanently maiming people rather than killing them is a deliberate attempt to drain a nation's economic and psychological resources; it has a far more deleterious economic and psychological impact on community life than simply killing them as: 'disabled people remain far more visible than the dead' (Coleridge 1993: 107).

Despite these difficulties a recent UN report (Despouy 1993) has suggested that there are more than 500 million impaired persons in the world; that is one in ten of the world's population. The report goes on to suggest that at least '25 per cent of the entire population are adversely affected by the presence of disabilities'. Not everyone would agree with this figure, however, including those international agencies who have responsibility for collecting the appropriate data.

The ten per cent figure has in any case now been discounted by WHO itself. The author of the WHO Manual on Community-Based Rehabilitation, Dr Hillender, who was responsible for declaring 10 per cent to be the world average, now favours about 4 per cent for developing countries and 7 per cent for developed countries.

(Coleridge 1993: 108)

Such figures are probably little better than guess work. There are obviously differences between the minority 'developed' and majority 'developing' worlds in both the kinds of impairments produced and the creation of disability that follows (Oliver 1990; Ingstad and Reynolds Whyte 1995). This uncertainty continues to exist despite the investment of large sums of money to produce a classification system to allow for accurate estimates of numbers (Wood 1980). Unfortunately this feeds into the policy-making process and produces inappropriate responses at international as well as national and local levels.

Conclusion

In this chapter we have argued that attempts to classify and count disabled people as an aid to policy-making have failed. The reasons for this failure are made absolutely clear by Paul Abberley (1996) who, over the years, has been a major critic of government number-crunching based on the ICIDH. Such a project is an impossible one, since:

'disability' is a social construct, and definitions are inevitably contested. They depend on the interests, intentions and unexamined presuppositions of those with the power to define, and the ability of those so defined to resist inappropriate conceptions of our reality.

(Abberley 1996: 182)

Nevertheless, we have suggested that social research can still have an important role to play in ending the exclusion of disabled people from their societies and communities across the globe, by including disabled people in the processes of definition and classification. Our recent partial inclusion has begun to produce the basis for programmes of barrier removal across the world and offers the potential for building an inclusionary world.

We should not get carried away, however, because the broad sweep of policy developments often take place with little reference to definitions and classifications in any case. In the next chapter we consider the ways in which history and culture, rather than definitions and social analysis, structure our understandings of the real nature of disability.

CHAPTER 3

Disability in history and culture

Introduction

To fully appreciate the experience of disability in current society and social policy as a response to it, an understanding of history and its relationship to culture is vital. Indeed, there is little doubt that current perceptions and responses are influenced by history and culture and that although there is growing evidence that these responses to impairment are by no means universal, there is clear evidence of a consistent bias against people with perceived impairments in Western culture throughout recorded history.

In this chapter we look at historical and cultural variations in the exclusionary/inclusionary processes in respect of disabled people, and show how they are continuing to exert an influence on welfare policy. The chapter is divided into three distinct but interrelated parts. The first examines cultural variations in perceptions of people with impairments. The second looks at social responses to impairment in Western culture before industrialisation with particular emphasis on developments in Britain. The third examines the material and ideological changes associated with the nineteenth and first half of the twentieth centuries.

Cultural variations

The existence of impairment is as old as the human body and in the earliest known societies it is a 'human constant' (Scheer and Groce 1989: 23). From at least the Neanderthal period onward, archaeologists have documented the regular appearance of individuals who would today be regarded as disabled people. Two notable examples are the skeleton of an elderly Neanderthal man with an advanced state of arthritis, an amputated arm, and a head injury found in Shanidar Cave, Iraq (Solecki 1971) and the remains of a teenage boy with 'severe' spina bifida, a congenital condition of the spine often resulting in the inability to walk, from the early Archaic Windover site in Florida, America, which dates back about 5000 years (Dickel and Doran 1989).

But while we have no idea of the prevalence of impairment in early societies – some conditions such as sensory and/or intellectual impairments, for example, would not be visible in skeletal remains – there is substantial evidence from north America, Europe, Egypt, China and Peru covering thousands of years of human history showing that the incidence of impairment was common among our ancestors (Ackernecht 1971).

These examples suggest that even the earliest societies were able to include impaired people within them and that they did not necessarily resort to the most extreme form of social exclusion, notably death. Despite these and other examples, one of the earliest and certainly one of the most influential explanations for the exclusion of disabled people is the 'surplus population thesis'.

As we shall see, an inevitable development of late-nineteenth century European thinking – notably, liberal utilitarianism and social Darwinism – it argues that in societies where economic survival is precarious any weak or dependent individuals will be disposed of. Hence, children with impairments are killed, adults with acquired impairments are forced out of the community, and elderly people are left to die. For instance, in a study of Eskimo society conducted at the turn of the century Rasmussen (1908) gives an example of an Eskimo man and his wife severely injured in an explosion; unable to fend for themselves, the woman is left to die while the man commits suicide.

The main problem with this analysis is that there are many examples of communities where economic survival is extremely hazardous, yet people with impairments remain valued members of the community. Two examples are the Dalegura, a group of Australian Aborigines (Hastings 1918–1921), and the Palute, a tribe of native Americans (Hanks and Hanks 1980). In both societies infanticide was prohibited, age was considered a sign of authority and respect, and individuals with impairments were not abandoned. Indeed: 'in the Dalegura tribe, a woman, a cripple from birth, was carried about by the tribespeople in turns, until her death at the age of sixty six' (Hastings 1918–1921: 443).

Another approach to the exclusion of disabled people is rooted in the work of Mary Douglas (1966) and Robert Murphy (1987). Responding to deep-rooted psychological fears of the unknown, Douglas argues that 'primitive' cultures react to 'anomalies' such as impairment by reducing it, physically controlling it, avoiding it, labelling it dangerous or adopting it as ritual (Douglas 1966: 39–40). For Douglas impairment is a problem; it is not part of the human condition or experience. Similarly, Robert Murphy utilises Victor Turner's (1967) concept of 'liminality' to explain the position of people with impairments in all societies. Thus, disabled people live in a state of social suspension, neither ' "sick" nor "well", "dead" nor "alive", "out of society nor wholly in it . . . they exist in partial isolation from society as undefined, ambiguous people" ' (Murphy 1987: 112).

This approach, focusing as it does on exclusion as solely a cultural phenomenon, has become increasingly popular in explaining exclusionary processes across a range of excluded groups, leading some social theorists to begin to talk about 'the universal other'. Influenced by postmodernist theory they often seem unaware that the use of such a category is dependent on accepting both a metanarrative and a dualistic approach to social theory.

There are other difficulties with this approach too. One, as we have already seen, is that not all societies respond to impairment negatively. Two, this essentially phenomenological perspective reduces explanations for cultural phenomena such as perceptions of physical, sensory and intellectual difference to the level of thought processes and metaphysics, thus detracting attention away from economic and social considerations.

A further problem relates to the fact that if we accept that attitudes toward people with impairments are somehow psychologically based then there is little that we can do about them; therefore, the social oppression of disabled people will always be with us. This is clearly not the case: even in Western societies, attitudes toward disabled people have changed dramatically over the last decade or so.

While we are not denying the importance of either economic circumstances or culture in shaping exclusionary processes, neither surplus population nor 'universal other' approaches capture the complexities of the relationship between the two. A more plausible explanation stems from the work of Hanks and Hanks. In a much overlooked anthropological review, first published in 1948 and republished in 1980, they demonstrate that cultural responses to people with impairments in non-Western societies are highly variable and determined by a wide range of factors.

In sociological terms, these can be divided into two distinct but interrelated categories: namely, the mode of production and the central value system. The former includes the type of economy, the need for and the type of labour, the amount of surplus it generates and the way it is distributed. The latter relates to the social structure: whether hierarchical or egalitarian, how achievement is defined, perceptions of age and sex, its relations with neighbouring societies, its aesthetic values 'and many more functionally related factors' (Hanks and Hanks 1980: 13).

Clearly, social responses to impairment cannot be explained simply with reference to single factors such as the economy or culture. They are culturally produced through the complex interaction between 'the mode of production and the central values of the society concerned' (Oliver 1990: 34). We now focus on the history of social responses to people with impairments in Western society with particular emphasis on the British experience – the birthplace of industrial capitalism (Marx 1970).

The origins of disability

Until the seventeenth century, despite the harshness of living conditions, most people were included in their village communities even if they were subjected to controlling measures such as the pillar and the stocks and even ridicule. Exclusion from the community was unusual and those people rejected by their families and without resources relied on the haphazard and often ineffectual tradition of Christian charity for subsistence. People with 'severe' impairments were usually herded together in one of the very small medieval hospitals in which were gathered 'the poor, the sick and the bedridden'. The ethos of these establishments was ecclesiastical rather than medical (Scull 1984).

But during the sixteenth century the wealth and power of the English Church was greatly reduced because of a series of unsuccessful political confrontations with the Crown. There was also a steady growth in the numbers of people dependent on charity. This was the result of a growing population following depletion caused by plagues, successive poor harvests and an influx of immigrants from Ireland and Wales (Stone 1985).

This prompted a fear of 'bands of sturdy beggars' among local dignitaries and magistrates who demanded an appropriate response from the central authority: the Crown (Trevelyan 1948). The Tudor monarchs responded by making economic provision for those hitherto dependent on the Church. The Poor Law of 1601, therefore, represents the first official recognition of the need for state intervention in the lives of people with perceived impairments.

But a general suspicion of people claiming charity had already been established by the statute of 1388 which mandated local officials to discriminate between the 'deserving' and the 'undeserving' poor. Yet while people with impairments were among the 'deserving poor', there was little attempt to separate them from the rest of the community. On the contrary, every effort was made to keep them within the local environment.

Although there was some parochial variation in terms of the actual level of support, there was a degree of uniformity in the way disabled people were treated. The lion's share of resources was directed toward 'domestic' or 'household relief' for people who were regarded as unable to work and were confined to the home. Funds were frequently provided to individuals and families willing to accept responsibility for people considered to be incapable of looking after themselves (Stone 1985). Major changes to this essentially inclusionary or 'community care' type policy did not begin to be discussed or implemented until the nineteenth century.

So while economic and social conditions were a key influence shaping society's response to disabled people, the Church remained a formidable force in English and European culture. Besides offering forgiveness and a democratic afterlife in a frequently hostile world, where for many life could be 'nasty, brutish and short' (Hobbes 1983), the Christian Church asserted and retained its authority by propagating and perpetuating fear: fear of the Devil and of his influence. The Biblical link between impairment, impurity and sin was central to this process.

People with perceived impairments provided living proof of Satan's existence and of his power over humans. Visibly impaired children were seen as 'changelings' – the Devil's substitutes for human children. The Malleus Maleficarum of 1487 declared that such 'creatures' were the result of their mothers' involvement with sorcery and witchcraft. The religious leader and scholar accredited with the formation of the Protestant reformation, Martin Luther (1485–1546), proclaimed he saw the Devil in a visibly disabled child. They were 'more obnoxious than ten children with their crapping, eating and screaming', Luther believed that they should be killed (Haffter 1968).

As in the ancient world (Garland 1995), these beliefs were reflected in medieval literature and art. Probably the most famous example is Shakespeare's *Richard the Third*, written in the late-sixteenth century. Although there is no evidence that Richard had any physical impairments, Shakespeare portrays him as twisted in both body and mind: since he cannot succeed as a lover because of his deformity he is determined to succeed as a villain. This essentially distorted and inherently negative view of disabled people is evident in a great deal of literature and art, both classical and popular, and continues to be produced today.

People with impairments were also primary targets for amusement and ridicule during the middle ages. Keith Thomas' (1977) analysis of the joke books of Tudor and Stuart England clearly illustrates the extent of this dimension of the oppression encountered by disabled people during this time. Besides references to the other so-called timeless universals of 'popular' humour such as foreigners, women and the clergy:

Every disability from idiocy to insanity to diabetes and bad breath was a welcome source of amusement, 'we jest at a man's body that is not well proportioned' said Thomas Wilson, '. . . and laugh at his countenance . . . if it be not comely by nature'. A typical Elizabethan joke book contains 'merry jests at fools' and merry jests at 'blind folk'. While some of the tricksters pranks are brutal to the extreme.

(Thomas 1977: 80–81)

Moreover, children and adults with obvious impairments were often displayed at village fairs (Nicholli 1990), visits to Bedlam were a common form of amusement for the able but ignorant, and the practice of keeping 'idiots' as objects of entertainment was prevalent among the aristocracy (Ryan and Thomas 1987). As we shall see, disabled people are the focus for much of what passes for comedy today.

Industrialisation and after

The coming of the eighteenth century brought with it an intensification of the commercialisation of land and agriculture, and the beginnings of industrialisation. It also witnessed the emergence of the Enlightenment giving rise to a range of progressive ideas including a critique of established religions, an emphasis on the value of reason and 'science', a commitment to social progress and the significance of individuality. Taken together these economic and cultural developments provided a legitimacy for developing policies of exclusion, although they built on the culture and practices from earlier times.

Hence, throughout the eighteenth and nineteenth centuries the policy of segregating people with impairments into institutional settings slowly increased and was subsequently extended to other disadvantaged groups. Although the term 'institution' can be used to refer to a variety of social organisations ranging from the family to a university, in this particular instance it refers to any long-term provision of a highly organised kind on a residential basis with the expressed aims of 'care', 'treatment' or 'custody' (Jones and Fowles 1984).

One explanation for this apparent break from inclusionary policies towards exclusion links it to the breakdown of early forms of state welfare in the face of large-scale urban industrialisation and the inevitable spread of poverty which followed (Rothman 1971). But the impetus to build institutions came before the growth of cities and was more pronounced in rural communities (Scull 1984). A variation on this theme, however, suggests that the widespread incarceration of people with impairments is linked to the transition from agriculture and cottage-based industries to factory-based systems:

> The speed of factory work, the enforced discipline, the time keeping and production norms, all these were a highly unfavourable change from the slower, more self-determined and flexible methods of work into which many handicapped people had been integrated.
>
> (Ryan and Thomas 1987: 101)

Although these arguments tend to play down the general antipathy surrounding impairment before the industrial revolution, clearly the economic and social conditions created by industrialisation, especially the spread of waged labour, compounded the difficulties faced by people with impairments. First, a family solely reliant on waged labour could not provide for all its members during economic depression, so large groups of dependent people were created by industrialisation. Second, the Elizabethan system of Poor Law relief was directly at odds with the needs of the burgeoning free market economy. Waged labour made the distinction between the 'able-bodied' and non-able bodied poor crucially important because local relief for the latter radically interfered with the need for labour mobility.

Segregating the poor into institutions, on the other hand, had several advantages over domestic relief: it was efficient, it acted as a major deterrent to the able-bodied 'malingerer' and it could instil good work habits into the inmates. These conclusions are clearly reflected in the Report of the Poor Law Commission and the Poor Law Amendment Act 1834. The 1834 reforms introduced three new principles for state welfare policy: national uniformity, denial of relief outside an institution, and deterrence as the basis for setting the levels of welfare benefits (Stone 1996). Thus, exclusion, both as physical coercion and as ideological threat, was to become the major driver of social policy in the nineteenth century.

Deterrence was evident in the principle of 'least eligibility' which stated that a pauper's situation should be less comfortable than that of an 'independent labourer of the lowest class' before benefits could be granted. The workhouse was intended to be as unpleasant as possible so that no one would enter it willingly. Families were broken up, inmates were made to wear specific uniforms, there were no recreational facilities and socialising was strictly forbidden in working hours. Routines were rigidly enforced and food was limited to what was considered necessary for survival and work.

The nineteenth century was also significant for an upsurge of Christian morality and 'humanitarian' values which was to have a profound effect on the lives of disabled people. A mixture of religious altruism and conscience, this spirit of Victorian patronage called into question the widespread though unexposed practice of infanticide for impaired children (Tooley 1983). It also stimulated some Victorians to question the harsh treatment meted out to people who were generally considered to be incapable of finding work.

Combined with the well-established mistrust of people claiming charity, these philanthropic ideals set in motion a process of differentiation which not only separated people with impairments from other disadvantaged sections of the community, but also divided them up into specific categories and groups with differing treatments for each group. The exclusionary process was becoming ever more complex and sophisticated and was beginning to necessitate the use of 'experts' to properly operationalise it.

From the outset the Poor Law Commission decreed that workhouses should separate the incarcerated population into four different groups: able-bodied males, able-bodied females, children and the deserving poor, and the 'aged and infirm'. The latter were housed in different buildings and accorded different treatment. Later, with the aid of the burgeoning medical profession, they were divided into four sub groups: the 'aged and infirm', the 'sick', the 'insane', and 'defectives' (Stone 1985).

The oldest of the four categories, the 'aged and infirm', referred to people with chronic illness and/or permanent impairments. While there was little official controversy over their eligibility for outdoor relief, they were usually directed into an institutional setting. The term 'sick' referred to anyone with acute, temporary or infectious diseases. Such people automatically qualified for outdoor relief, but where incarceration was unavoidable separate accommodation was provided, although conditions in these facilities were rarely better than those in the workhouse. Illness could not be seen as a route to better treatment or it would discourage poor people from making provision for the future and thus undermine the prevailing philosophy of self-reliance.

People described as 'insane' were singled out for special treatment from the outset. Despite the difficulties of definition and diagnosis, there was already a universal recognition of the 'problem' of people with intellectual impairments. There were two main strategies for dealing with it. 'Idiots', 'lunatics', the 'mad' or 'persons suffering from diseases of the brain' were either admitted to an asylum or boarded out on contract to families who would be responsible for them (Scull 1984). Several private asylums had been established in the seventeenth century. But public outcries over the atrocious conditions found in many of these establishments brought to light by Evangelical reformers forced the government into setting up a state-run system in 1845. It is important to note, however, that the cruelty accorded people perceived as mentally ill inside institutions was often no worse than that which they encountered in the community at large (Roth and Kroll 1986).

Until 1871 Poor Law officials had no right to detain people in an institution against their will, but this did not apply to those termed insane. Prior to the Lunacy Legislation of 1845, the certification of insanity was the responsibility of local lay officials. Following that date, confirmation of 'mental illness' was valid only if a doctor was involved. This change has been attributed to doctors' assertions that mental illness has physiological causes, is responsive to medical treatment, and their successful struggle for control within private and public institutions (Scull 1984). Once defined as 'mentally ill' an individual could be detained on a doctor's recommendation and moved from one institution to another against their will. Doctors still retain this power. Hence, 1845 can be seen as the start of the medical profession's subsequent domination of all aspects of 'disability' (Barnes 1990, 1991).

The term 'defectives' was used to describe people with sensory impairments such as blindness, deafness or the lack of speech. After 1903 people with epilepsy and children hitherto termed 'mentally subnormal' were also added to this category. Although this group were still liable to be put into an institution, and their treatment therein was no different to that of other inmates, they were frequently singled out for special attention by Victorian philanthropists and charities. Many of the charities which exist today were founded during this period. For example, the British and Foreign Association for Promoting the Education of the Blind (the forerunner to The Royal National Institute for the Blind (RNIB) was formed in 1863 (RNIB 1990).

As the nineteenth century drew to a close the pressures to incarcerate people so classified increased dramatically. First, the transition from relatively light industries such as textiles to the much heavier capital goods industries like iron, steel and the railways, in what has been called the 'second phase of industrialization' (Hobsbawn 1968), further emphasised the importance of physical fitness as a criterion for finding work among working people. Second, welfare policies, particularly with regard to outdoor relief, were severely tightened during the 1870s and 1880s because of escalating costs caused by rising unemployment following a decade of economic depression which began with the severe winter of 1860/61. This put more pressure on local authorities to apply the 'workhouse test' to anyone seeking welfare. Third, there was a further expansion of segregated institutions for the deserving poor following public scandals and government enquiries exposing the appalling conditions in workhouses. The numbers of disabled people consigned to these establishments rose accordingly. They did not began to fall until the late 1950s (Scull 1984; Humphries and Gordon 1992).

As mentioned above, ideological legitimacy for these policies is evident in the ascendant Enlightenment philosophies of the period which stressed the rights and privileges of the individual over and above those of the group or state in relation to property rights, politics and culture.

'Scientific' authenticity for these ideas was reinforced in 1857 with the publication of Charles Darwin's *The Origin of Species*. Clearly influenced by the evolutionary themes of Thomas Malthus' *Essay on Population*, first published in 1798, it explains biological development in terms of natural selection and the survival of the fittest. For Darwin, evolution is progress and inevitably beneficial.

These ideas had an understandable appeal to a society dominated by a relatively small élite of property-owning, self-interested, rational individuals who welcomed any opportunity to justify their newly acquired wealth, status and power. Hence, they were quickly applied to human development. What later became known as 'Social Darwinism' dispelled and allayed the qualms of the rich about not helping the disadvantaged by assuring them that the latter's deprivations were the inevitable price of progress, which could only be resolved through the struggle for existence.

Out of the general tendency to apply Darwin's theories to human affairs emerged the eugenics movement. Concerned mainly with what they saw as racial degeneration through the birth of 'defective' children, the eugenicists reiterated ancient fears that disabled people were a serious threat to British and European society. The work of Francis Galton (1869), Darwin's cousin, and the statistician who coined the term 'eugenics', R. L. Dugdale (1877) and Henry Goddard (1912) reinforced traditional myths that there were genetic links between physical and mental impairments, crime, unemployment and other social evils.

The stated aim of the eugenicists was to improve the British race by preventing the reproduction of 'defectives' by sterilisation and segregation (Kevles 1985). In effect, what they had managed to do was provide a rational and scientific legitimation for the existing policies of excluding disabled people. This could be done by death-making, sterilisation and incarceration encompassing rigid segregation of the sexes.

Inevitably, by the turn of the century prejudice was rife. The stigma of 'feeble-mindedness' or 'mental deficiency' had become firmly embedded in the public mind. In 1896 the 'National Association for the Care and Control of the Feeble-Minded' was set up as a pressure group for the lifetime segregation of disabled people. During the 1910 general elections they campaigned vigorously on these issues. Disabled women were singled out for particular attention. In 1912 one commentator noted:

Feeble-minded women are almost invariably immoral and if at large usually become carriers of venereal disease or give birth to children twice as defective as themselves.

(Cited in Potts and Fido 1991: 10)

It is within this context that the Mental Deficiency Act of 1913 came into force. It reflected the general view that society should be protected from the evils of impairment and abnormality. Thus, the diagnosis 'mental deficiency', especially when supported by the whole array of 'scientific' statistical procedures assembled by Galton and others, became convincing evidence for the removal of the 'afflicted from free society' (Radford 1994: 15).

In the following two decades eugenic fears were further endorsed by the widespread use of intelligence quotient (IQ) tests in British schools. Their inventors, the French psychologists Binet and Simon, and principal advocates, such as the psychologist Cyril Burt, asserted confidently that intelligence is innate and that the majority of defectives were ineducable. Yet despite the fact that there are serious doubts about the validity of such tests, as they measure only a comparatively small range of human qualities, the nature of which are culturally determined, similar techniques are still used today to separate the 'normal' from the 'subnormal'.

Eugenic fears were prevalent throughout the 1920s and 1930s. The Report of the Departmental Committee on Sterilisation chaired by Lord Brock recommended legislation to ensure the 'voluntary' sterilisation of 'mentally defective women' (Ryan and Thomas 1987). Although never actually passed in Britain, similar legislation became law in several other Western democracies including America. By 1938, 33 American states had a sterilisation law and nationwide over 27 000 compulsory operations had been performed (Pfeiffer 1994).

But eugenic ideals reached their logical conclusion in 1930s and 1940s Germany when the Nazi party systematically murdered 200 000 disabled people whom they labelled 'life unworthy of life' (Burleigh 1994). It was here that the real and inevitable consequence of exclusionary social policies towards disabled people reached its zenith.

It is important to remember too that Marxist communism has its roots in the nineteenth century and, indeed, many of its main protagonists embraced eugenic ideals as a corollary of the 'Utopian' hope for a better society. Prominent leaders of the socialist Fabian society, for example, such as Beatrice and Sidney Webb, George Bernard Shaw, and H. G. Wells were enthusiastic eugenicists. Furthermore, these ideas persisted well into the late-twentieth century, enabling so-called socialist leaders throughout the world to advocate birth control and sterilisation in the pursuit of social development (DAA 1995; Kevles 1985; Stone 1996).

Inevitably such perceptions are reflected in nineteenth and early-twentieth century literature and culture. By 1850 Britain had a well-established publishing industry providing a wide range of titles for both the domestic and overseas markets including the British Empire and the USA. In Queen Victoria's reign, over 40 000 novels were published, some in several editions. The spread of libraries helped to make novels, periodicals and works of non-fiction widely available throughout society. Initially, much of the material produced was of a highly philanthropic nature – particularly that which was aimed at children.

People with perceived impairments were presented not as a group but as 'other', inexorably trapped in their condition. Impairment could not be understood in human terms but as with all 'human suffering' placed firmly within 'God's scheme of things'.

Disabled people are a reminder that we are merely (and undeservingly) lucky if we are not disabled; that we are our brother's keepers; and that they must evoke in non-disabled people compassion in feeling and action.

(Davidson *et al*. 1994: 43)

The age-old tendency of presenting disabled people as objects of curiosity and/or ridicule found expression in the travelling fairs, carnivals and 'freak shows' which flourished throughout Britain and north America in the nineteenth and early part of the twentieth century. Here people with any kind of overt abnormality, such as Joseph Merrick, 'The Elephant Man', for example, were put on display for the general public's amazement, amusement and, of course, to reaffirm their sense of normality. But although these exhibitions were frequently the site for the uncontrolled exploitation and degradation of people with impairments, for some they provided a welcome refuge from the pathologising gaze and controlling influence of the newly ascendant medical profession (Bogdan 1988; Darke 1994). As we shall see, the consequences of this cultural legacy of exclusion remain with us today.

Conclusion

This chapter has provided a brief history of disability in Western society. We have shown that while social responses to impairment are by no means universal, there has been a consistent cultural bias against people with impairments throughout recorded history, and that this phenomenon is attributable to both material and cultural forces. Moreover, although the philosophical and cultural foundations upon which the social oppression of disabled people rests were firmly entrenched in the ancient world of Greece and Rome, they were substantially reinforced by the economic and social upheavals of the eighteenth and nineteenth centuries.

The growing importance of economic rationality, individualism and medical science during this period contributed to and compounded ancient fears and prejudices concerning perceived impairments, and provided intellectual legitimacy for relatively more extreme discriminatory policies and practices: notably, the systematic removal of disabled people from the mainstream of economic and social life.

We have argued that in the nineteenth and early-twentieth century, state policy became exclusionary in respect of disabled people and that this exclusion was both shaped by and reflected in the dominant culture. In the next chapter we examine the way social policy has developed in the later-twentieth century and look at the way in which it has compounded rather than challenged the exclusionary practices of yesteryear despite a shift to what we might call 'a culture of inclusion' or the perhaps more familiar term 'community care'.

CHAPTER 4

What policies exist?

Introduction

The category 'disability' as we know it today did not come into existence until the eighteenth century, although as we have already argued impaired people have always existed. Leonard Davis (1995) explains:

the social process of disabling arrived with industrialisation and with a set of practices and discourses that are linked to late eighteenth- and nineteenth-century notions of nationality, race, gender, criminality, sexual orientation and so on.

(Davis 1995: 24)

According to this argument, disability has become a socially constructed category. Thus, as Harlan Hahn has argued about current policy: 'Fundamentally, disability is defined by public policy. In other words, disability is whatever policy says it is' (Hahn 1985: 294). While, in a sense this may be true, the existence of impaired people since the dawn of time has posed economic and social dilemmas for societies and not merely conceptual ones.

What is of concern to us here are the ways in which economic, social and cultural forces have been reflected in disability policy and the ways such policies may change over time. We suggested in the last chapter that welfare policy in Britain was operated largely within the exclusionary principle, at least until the end of the Second World War when, according to Anthony Giddens:

The new welfare policies were designed to treat all citizens as part of a more inclusive national order and in so doing to recognise state responsibility for caring for those who were in some way prevented from active economic participation.

(Giddens 1996: 65)

While there is no doubt that at the level of ideology the inclusionary approach was adopted, whether this has actually resulted in the inclusion of disabled people into mainstream society is another matter. In this chapter we look at the rise and fall of what has sometimes been called the classic welfare state, examine the outcomes it has produced for disabled people, and suggest that despite its intentions the whole project has continued to exclude because of the way it has constructed disabled people.

The classic welfare state

The British welfare state, as we know it today, emerged from the economic and political uncertainty during and immediately after the Second World War and is perceived as part of the postwar settlement between capital and labour. Whatever it was, it created an almost universal approach to the issue of social policy and was intended to provide cradle-to-grave security to all the citizens of Britain. Within this essentially universalistic approach, certain groups such as 'children, the elderly, the mentally ill and the disabled' were to be provided with specific services, whereas other groups such as families, women, and people from minority ethnic groups merited little if any serious consideration.

Certainly disabled people were no longer to be treated simply as subcategories of broader policy initiatives as they had been in the past. Coupled with the inclusionary approach, this recognition of disabled people as a specific group promised much, as did this newly emerging welfare state to the rest of society – but that is a broader story than we are able to articulate here.

The first Act of Parliament to treat disabled people as a single group was the Disabled Persons (Employment) Act 1944 which attempted to secure employment rights for disabled people (Topliss 1982). Further, the Education Act 1944, underpinned by an egalitarian ideology, specified that disabled children should be educated alongside their non-disabled peers in primary and secondary education (Tomlinson 1982). The National Assistance Act 1948 laid a duty on local authorities to arrange a variety of services for disabled people, both in the community and institutions. The National Health Service Act 1948 also provided hospital-based treatment and long-term care for disabled people (Oliver 1983).

However, it soon became clear that implementation of the Disabled Persons (Employment) Act was more concerned with not upsetting employers than ensuring that disabled people seeking employment were treated fairly. The Education Act became the legal mechanism for the establishment of a huge infrastructure of segregated special education based around 11 medical categories. The National Assistance Act allowed but did not require local authorities to provide services, and the choice for many disabled people was either to survive without assistance or go into residential care. The National Health Service Act offered little beyond acute treatment, and long-term care usually meant living on a 'geriatric' ward even when the individuals concerned were not beyond retirement age (Barnes 1991; Oliver and Barnes 1993).

While the intention behind these policies was undoubtedly inclusionary, it quickly became apparent that the newly established infrastructure of services was not doing what it was intended to do. Despite the legislation, disabled people were not being included in the key institutions of mainstream society such as work and education, and the old exclusionary practices often carried on unchanged and largely unchallenged. Even those people ostensibly living in the community received little or no support from the state and remained excluded from society, albeit living unsupported within their families (Campbell and Oliver 1996; Humphries and Gordon 1992).

By the late 1950s policy-makers had come to recognise that their inclusionary intentions had not been realised for specific groups, including disabled people, and there was a concerted attempt by successive governments to reduce the numbers of people living in segregated institutions of one kind or another. The shift towards community-based services took a decisive turn in the early 1960s when the government announced its intention to reduce the number of beds in psychiatric hospitals by half: a move which prompted a number of critics to argue that the motives behind this change in policy were economic rather than humanitarian. One commentator, Richard Titmus, challenged the government to refute this allegation, but there was no official reply. In 1962 the Ministry of Health published *A Hospital Plan*. This was followed one year later by *Health and Welfare: The Development of Community Care*, generally referred to as *The Community Care Blue Book*.

The origins of the use of the phrase 'community care' can be found in the Report of the Royal Commission on Mental Deficiency of 1954/57, which considered the problems arising from outdated mental hospitals and the stigma associated with in-patient treatment. Although no precise definition was given, subsequent government statements and documents on services for disabled people have increasingly used the term. But before proceeding further, it is important to remember the exclusionary implications of the phrase itself. The concept 'community' is a hazy one, but within the context of community care it suggests life outside an institution within a bounded locality characterised by close social networks between neighbours and friends. Broadly speaking the word 'care' means to be looked after and protected. It carries with it definite implications of dependence and is widely used in relation to children and acutely ill or very frail older people. What is actually meant by the term 'community care' is community dependence or, to be more accurate, dependence on the community. Moreover, when applied to disabled people it implies that they are unable to take control of their own lives (Rae 1990).

However, *A Hospital Plan* and *Health and Welfare: The Development of Community Care* provided a sketchy outline of plans for community-based services. These included proposals for increases in the numbers of general practitioners, home helps, district nurses, health visitors, sheltered housing schemes and sheltered workshops. Provision was intended for four specific groups, namely 'mothers and children, the elderly, the mentally disordered and the physically handicapped'. Around this time a number of critical investigations into institutional life by social scientists were published (see for example Barton 1959; Goffman 1961; Townsend 1967; Miller and Gwynne 1972). There were also a spate of sensational public expositions of the cruelty and harsh treatment manifest in institutions for older people and those with severe emotional distress. All were subsequently investigated and in one particular case, the Ely enquiry, criminal proceedings were brought against hospital personnel (Jones *et al.* 1983).

As a result of these enquiries, public and in some cases professional confidence in the services provided in long-stay hospitals and similar establishments was again seriously undermined. Local authority services, on the other hand, remained relatively unscathed and underdeveloped. Consequently the pressure to reduce the numbers of people in institutions run by the health service intensified while local authorities were encouraged to expand their facilities accordingly. But there was little agreement as to what services should be provided or where the money to fund the expansion should come from.

Extensive variation characterised provision at the local level and budgets were already stretched because of two main factors. The first was the rising expectations of the general population after the setting up of the welfare state; the second, a steady increase in the numbers of 'dependent' people after the Second World War. These included children, people over retirement age and, of course, disabled people. Nonetheless, the rhetoric of community care obscured the reality that for many previously incarcerated people, living in the community bestowed no more rights other than perhaps to starve, freeze or die alone.

By the late 1960s attempts were being made to rationalise the chaos that was the reality of community care. In an effort to develop provision at the local level the government set up a commission of enquiry which published its findings in 1968. *The Seebohm Report* is generally considered a watershed in the development of community-based services for disabled people. Among its principal conclusions were the recommendations that local authorities should accumulate data relating to the nature and size of the problems associated with disability, and that they should develop and/or expand services in conjunction with those already provided by the health service and the voluntary sector.

These recommendations were subsequently incorporated into the Local Authority Act 1970 and the Chronically Sick and Disabled Persons Act (CSDP) 1970. Indeed, the CSDP Act was supposed to be the vehicle for service rationalisation. It was even heralded at one point by two non-disabled commentators, Eda Topliss and Bryan Gould (1981), as a 'Charter (of rights) for the disabled' but the reality was that it was merely an extension of the needs-based welfare provision of the National Assistance Act 1948 (Keeble 1979). In fact the only two extra duties that were to be imposed on local authorities were one, the duty to compile a register and two, the duty to publicise services. The former produced little information of value and the latter was widely ignored (Knight and Warren 1978). The services listed under Section 2 only needed to be provided where it was 'practical and reasonable' to do so, and for most local authorities it 'wasn't so they didn't' (Cook and Mitchell 1982; Keep and Clarkson 1993).

Local government was reorganised at the same time, creating community-based social service departments; and all this change certainly signalled a switch in welfare state personnel into community-based welfare bureaucracies. The problem for disabled people was that these changes did not provide them with supported community living through inclusionary practice but continued to offer them the same old choice: ensure your own inclusion through your own efforts or risk exclusion by being forced into residential care.

Despite the rhetoric of integration, community care and rights which emerged in the 1980s, neither the Education Act 1981 nor the Disabled Persons (Services, Consultation and Representation) Act 1986 has significantly improved the quality of welfare services available to disabled people. The evidence for this continuing failure has been provided by officially commissioned government research showing the extent of poverty and unemployment among disabled people (Martin *et al.* 1989); studies by independent research institutes showing that disabled people are 'last on the list' as far as welfare services are concerned (Beardshaw 1988); academics who show that services to enable disabled people to live in the community are poor (Blaxter 1980; Borsay 1986); and disabled people who condemn health authorities and social service departments who fail to provide them with a satisfactory quality of life (Oliver *et al.* 1988; Morris 1989).

By the end of the 1980s it was clear that despite the establishment of a comprehensive legal framework for the provision of inclusionary services to disabled people, these services somehow do not get delivered (Barnes 1991; Oliver and Barnes 1993). The main reasons for this were first, services had been provided on the basis of professional definitions of need; second, governments of all political persuasion had consistently resisted pressure to force local authorities to meet their statutory obligations; and third, those services that have been provided have locked disabled people into dependency on them.

Rethinking community care and inclusionary practice

The problems with welfare services were not unique to disabled people and prompted a major review of the welfare state in the mid-1980s. This review signalled the breaking down of the postwar consensus over the welfare state and was prompted by increasing concerns about the costs of the classic welfare state whose main success appeared to be in socialising people into dependency. Beginning with a damning report on community care from the Audit Commission (1986), the Griffiths Report (1988) followed and in 1990, and after much delay, the review was included in a White Paper *Caring for People*. After a very short consultation period the White Paper was incorporated into the National Health Service and Community Care Act 1990.

Central to the new legislation was a new managerial strategy for providing services which was to be supplemented by a market strategy which involved stimulating the private and voluntary sectors to act as providers of services and for the statutory authorities to act as enablers and purchasers of services rather than sole providers. By opting for this combination of market and managerial strategies, the government hoped that the problems of professional dominance and dependency creation would be addressed.

However, such hopes were soon dashed, from the point of view of disabled people at least. Ken Davis comments on the continuing dominance of professionals over service delivery: 'At this juncture, our lives are substantially still in their hands. They still determine most decisions and their practical outcomes' (Davis 1993: 199). There is little evidence that disabled people are being involved in the planning and delivery of services in the way that legislation requires (Bewley and Glendinning 1992). Nor is there much evidence that local authority assessment procedures adequately reflect the legal requirement to place individual needs at the centre of the reforms (Ellis 1993). Finally, studies that have recently been carried out are not optimistic that the existing reforms are enough and unless further changes are made, as far as disabled people are concerned 'their opportunities to be independent citizens will disappear' (Morris 1993: 147).

The legislation has not changed the balance of power between professional and service user. It is now the care manager who assesses the needs of the service user. Users do now have rights to see and even contribute to their care plans, but they have no greater rights to service and still no access to legally enforceable grievance procedures. Although writing before the recent legislation (see Chapter 5) the situation described by Cohen remains unchanged:

> much the same groups of experts are doing much the same business as usual. The basic rituals incorporated into the move to the mind – taking case histories, writing social enquiry reports, constructing files, organising case conferences – are still being enacted.
>
> (Cohen 1985: 153)

In the post-1990 world, then, the same people, albeit with different job titles and perhaps in plusher buildings, are doing the same things to disabled people although it may now be called 'doing a needs-led assessment' or 'producing a care plan'. Ken Davis is clear that the newly emerging profession of care management will not provide the necessary structural reforms:

> it is simply not enough for brokers, care managers or any other agent to potter about in the existing mish-mash of inappropriate and inadequate services, with a view to helping individual disabled people to piece together some kind of survival plan for existing in a hostile world. We have been there too long.
>
> (Davis 1990: 14)

So the welfare state has not ensured either the rights and entitlements to inclusion for disabled people in the past, nor has the most recent restructuring appeared to change this disturbing situation. Services as they are currently being provided are unlikely to satisfy disabled people and fall far short of the demands made by disabled people from all over Europe. This is clearly evident in the following statement from a conference in Strasbourg to discuss disabled people's on-going struggle for independent living.

We demand social welfare systems that include personal assistance services that are consumer controlled and which allow various models of independent living for disabled people, regardless of their disability and income. We demand social welfare legislation which recognises these services as basic civil rights and which provide necessary appeal procedures.

(ENIL 1989: 1. Included in Part Two of this book.)

What does it all mean for disabled people?

Having told our version of the story of the development of welfare services in respect of disabled people, we now provide a brief review of the ways in which social policy legislation impacts on the lives of disabled people in the areas of education, employment, health and welfare, social security and housing. While each of these areas will be treated separately for analytical purposes, their impact on the lives of disabled people are cumulative and the story we tell is one of failure; despite an extensive range of services being in place, they are often inadequate or inappropriate and fail to ensure an acceptable quality of life for the majority of disabled people. In short, they fail to ensure the full inclusion of disabled people into their societies.

Educational policy for children and young people with impairments has been and remains dominated by the traditional individualistic medical approach to disability. This has resulted in the creation and development of a segregated 'special' education system which is presented as a necessary adjunct to the mainstream sector by its supporters, and a key element in the social oppression of disabled people by its critics. Although successive legislation in the post-1945 years has threatened its abolition, the special education system has continued to thrive.

While the Education Act 1981 attempted to shift the emphasis from a medical discourse to an educational one by changing the terminology and categories, it failed to alter the segregative structures and practices that underpinned and continue to underpin special education. The Act also failed to shift the balance of power away from education professionals in that while LEAs are bound by law to assess the 'special educational needs' (SEN) of disabled children, this is a very complicated process involving a variety of professionals which can take up to three years to complete (Audit Commission 1992). Presented as a form of positive action, the assessment of SEN is often used to place disabled children in separate groups, classes and schools. The 1988 OPCS disability survey, mentioned earlier, estimated that there are 360 000 disabled children under 16 in Britain. Over a third of those living in private households and nearly two-thirds living in residential homes are educated in segregated environments of one form or another (Meltzer et al. 1989).

Furthermore, although segregated provision began to decline during the 1980s, successive research by the Centre for Studies on Inclusive Education (CSIE) shows that this was only marginal (Swann 1992) and recent evidence suggests that this trend is now in reverse. In England, for example: 'In January 1992, the special school population went up to 88 952 pupils, or from 1.47% in 1991 to 1.49% of all 5–15 year old pupils' (Norwich 1994: 3).

The Disabled Persons (Employment Act) 1944 was centrally concerned to give disabled people certain legal rights to participate in the labour market but it was never properly enforced and despite widespread abuse, only 10 employers were ever prosecuted in the 52 years of its existence. Subsequently, however, government policy shifted heavily in favour of persuasion rather than enforcement and providing individual solutions by fitting disabled people for jobs rather than adapting jobs for disabled people. While this approach has undoubtedly benefited some disabled individuals, it has not solved the employment problems of the disabled population as a whole (Barnes 1991; Oliver 1991; Thornton and Lunt 1995).

Indeed, there is substantial statistical evidence of the level of disadvantage disabled people encounter in the modern labour market. Unemployment is significantly higher among disabled workers. Although the levels vary slightly depending on the definitions and measures used, research from both official and unofficial sources shows that disabled men and women are up to three times more likely to be without a job (Martin *et al.* 1989; Prescott Clarke 1990; Berthoud *et al.* 1993; Hyde 1996).

There is also evidence that unemployed disabled workers want paid work. Prescott Clarke (1990), for example, found that 22 per cent of 'occupationally handicapped' but 'economically active' men and women want to work. These rates were almost twice as high as those for economically active men and women in the general population. Furthermore, this estimate does not take into account those disabled people of working age living in residential institutions – the OPCS study put this figure at 84 000 – nor those termed 'discouraged workers'. These are disabled people who have given up looking for work because of the barriers encountered in the labour market, or because of the type of work they are likely to find (Barnes 1991).

All too often the only type of work disabled workers can find is poorly paid, low-skilled jobs which are both unrewarding and undemanding; the type of work widely referred to as 'underemployment' (Walker 1982). Disabled men earn about a quarter less than non-disabled counterparts (Prescott Clarke 1990; Berthoud *et al.* 1993; Hyde 1996). The difference between the earnings of disabled and non-disabled women workers is less than that of male peers. But this is because underemployment is generally much higher for women workers (Lonsdale 1990; EOC 1991). Underemployment is also characterised by a lack of promotion opportunities, and the under-utilisation of disabled people's skills and training once in work (RADAR 1993; Thornton and Lunt 1995).

Poverty has been an inevitable consequence of living with an impairment. In many ways, this is the direct outcome of disabled people's exclusion from mainstream employment. But it is also because the system of welfare payments paid to people perceived as incapable of work has never covered the full costs of living with impairment. This is inevitable in a market-led economy organised around the profit motive and wage labour because besides acting as a 'safety net' for those deemed unable to work, the quality of life available to people living on welfare benefits must also act as a deterrent to people considered able but idle. The nineteenth-century principle of less eligibility, discussed in the previous chapter, is a necessary constant in this type of economic environment.

Peter Townsend (1979) found that over half the households with a disabled member had incomes at or below the official poverty line: the point at which people are considered eligible for social security payments or 'income support'. Official recognition came a decade later with the OPCS disability surveys, although the report dealing specifically with income does not use the word 'poverty'. This, as Paul Abberley (1991) has noted, is probably due to political expediency and ongoing debates about definitions of absolute and relative poverty.

Nevertheless, the OPCS survey estimated that over three-quarters, 78 per cent – over half of whom are below retirement age – of Britain's 6.2 million disabled adults are dependent on social security benefits as their main source of income. In general, the income of households with a disabled member stands at less than three-quarters, 72 per cent, of those without a disabled member (Martin and White 1988). Disabled people are also poorer than their neighbours because their basic living costs are much higher.

Throughout the post-1945 period the expansion of social support services for disabled people has been shaped by the traditional assumption that people with impairments are unable to make basic decisions about their own individual service needs (Oliver 1990; Wood 1990; Barnes 1991; Morris 1993). This has had far-reaching negative implications since logic dictates that if they cannot assume responsibility for organising their own lives, they cannot assume the responsibilities of citizenship. Generally, services are provided directly to the disabled person only when they live alone and where there is 'evidence that such services are not delivered in a way which enables people to have control over their daily living activities nor are they enabled to play a role in the wider society' (Morris 1993: 27).

To make matters worse, community-based services continue to be provided by a bewildering array of agencies and organisations including health authorities, local authorities' social service departments (SSDs), charities and private agencies, and provision and availability continues to vary considerably in different parts of the country (Beardshaw 1988). Furthermore, the rhetoric of community care must not obscure the fact that many disabled people have little choice but to live in residential institutions. According to the OPCS survey, 422 000 disabled adults live in institutions (Martin *et al.* 1989). Of these, 20 per cent are below retirement age and most of this group are in homes for older people, psychiatric and geriatric hospitals, or simply 'ordinary' hospital wards (Harrison 1987; Fielder 1988; Morris 1993). Contrary to popular belief, there was a substantial growth in 'residential care' during the 1980s in both the public and the private sectors. Social security support for people living in private residential care rose from £10 million in 1979 to £1000 million in 1989 (HMSO 1989). And: 'most people find that, once in residential care, it is extremely difficult to move out' (Morris 1993: 59).

Official figures show that 60 per cent of all disabled adults need some form of personal and/or domestic help for tasks they cannot do themselves (Martin *et al.* 1989). Examples include help with getting out of bed, using the toilet, dressing, cooking, and cleaning the house. The vast majority of these people rely on 'informal carers' – family and friends and usually women – for this type of support and, as noted earlier, often to the economic and emotional disadvantage of all concerned. Supplementary services are often provided but these are usually a combination of statutory and voluntary systems, and delivery is never guaranteed.

Hence, people receiving this type of service cannot organise their daily lives in the same way as the rest of the community. Even elementary decisions such as when to get up or go to bed are restricted. Also, because of government efforts to reduce public spending, local authorities are operating against a backdrop of stringent financial cuts. Consequently, provision is increasingly limited to home-based support and 'becoming less and less available for anything but the most basic personal care tasks' (Kestenbaum 1995: 21).

Although there are over four and a quarter million disabled people with mobility-related impairments in Britain (Martin *et al.* 1988) there is currently only around 80 000 accessible homes (these are houses which disabled people can get in and out of, and live in with a minimum of help) in both the public and the private sectors. Also, many of these homes are set apart from 'normal' houses in 'special needs housing ghettos' where disabled people are cut off from their families, their friends and the non-disabled community as a whole. The lack of accessible housing makes it very difficult for disabled people to integrate into community life, both in terms of employment and socially. For example, although visiting friends is one of the most popular forms of relaxation in the UK, many disabled people do not have this option because the only homes they can enter are their own (Rowe 1990).

Disabled people and their families are also twice as likely to live in property owned by local authorities (LAs) than non-disabled peers. This is because, first, they are poorer than non-disabled people and less able to buy or rent houses in the private sector. Second, LAs are the main providers of accessible homes, as they have a statutory duty to cater for disabled people's housing needs under the 1970 CSDP Act. Private-sector landlords rarely provide accessible homes and the recent deregulation of rents makes this less likely still. Moreover, most accessible houses are not compatible with disabled people's needs. Because of mainly mistaken assumptions about disabled people's housing requirements, there is an acute shortage of accessible homes with more than one bedroom. Most disabled people have families and single disabled people often need two bedrooms to accommodate themselves and their personal assistant.

The 1980s witnessed a dramatic reduction in housebuilding generally, so fewer accessible homes are being built. Although the government have acknowledged this problem (DSS 1994) at present there are no plans to encourage either public or private housebuilders to build to accessible standards. The result of all this is that homelessness among disabled people has increased dramatically. Between 1980 and 1988, for example, it increased by 92 per cent, compared to 57 per cent among the general population (Morris 1990). Moreover, this estimate does not include those people living in institutions, hospitals, or with their parents because of the lack of accessible homes (Kestenbaum 1995).

In view of the shortage of accessible homes, adapting existing properties is often seen as a way of meeting disabled people's housing needs. Most LAs have no specific policy in this area because official directives on adapting inaccessible homes are unnecessarily complex and allow for considerable discretion at the local level. In most areas the number of house adaptations being funded is very small and many disabled people have to use their own limited resources to make their homes accessible. Hence, many live in homes which are only partially adapted and mobility may be limited to only one room. In a recent national survey, only 29 per cent of disabled people living in private households thought that they had all the house adaptations they required and tenants in private rented accommodation fared worse (Lamb and Layzell 1994).

Disability policy in other parts of the world

In the previous chapter we considered the ways in which disabled people were treated in different cultural contexts and at different points in history. Here we consider the policy responses that have been made in the late-twentieth century in other countries, though inevitably this must be brief and speculative as there are few if any comprehensive comparative studies available. While some would argue that there are different kinds of welfare state throughout the world (Esping-Andersen 1990; Crow 1997), we suggest that underpinning these differences, there is a dominant welfare discourse which continues to construct disabled people as dependent and therefore in need of care, despite the fact that bodies like the United Nations (UN) insist that disability is a matter of human rights.

However many disabled people there are (see Chapter 2), there are clearly enough to come to the attention of the United Nations General Assembly, who adopted the Declaration on the Rights of Disabled Persons in 1975, recommending that all international organisations and agencies should include provisions in their programmes to ensure the effective implementation of these rights and principles. Subsequently 1981 was proclaimed International Year of Disabled Persons with the motto 'Full participation and equality' although both the programme itself and its implementation throughout the world continued to operate within the dominant welfare framework.

In the following year the UN adopted the World Programme of Action which provided the guidelines for the Decade of Disabled Persons (1983–92) proclaimed by the General Assembly. This proclamation makes it clear that 'disabled people have the same rights as others in their societies and that it is the duty of governments to promote and protect these rights' (see Document G in Part Two) but again, these rights are usually to dependency-creating welfare services which are generally not delivered in any case.

As far as the European Community is concerned, similar uncertainties abound over the numbers of disabled people, although figures for the prevalence of disabled people suggest that approximately 10 per cent of the population of the Community are disabled, meaning that there were more than 30 million disabled people residing in Europe. Policy towards disabled people developed in a more limited way than with the UN. In the 1970s four discrete programme areas developed: an initial action programme to promote the vocational rehabilitation of disabled people; the European Social Fund; a range of supported housing projects; and a programme of activities in the research field. Hopes that such discrete initiatives might form part of a comprehensive social charter of fundamental social rights were dashed in 1989 when such a proposal was watered down to become a 'Community Charter of Basic Social Rights of Workers' (Daunt 1991).

However, it is clear that these programmes have also remained locked into dependency-creating welfare discourse which have not fundamentally addressed the social exclusion of disabled people throughout Europe. Further, organisations of disabled people throughout Europe have become increasingly angry about the lack of involvement of disabled people in the planning and delivery of these programmes in the first place (see Document D in Part Two).

It is difficult to write about the relationship between citizenship and disability in the countries which used to be known as the 'Eastern Block'. What evidence we do have suggests that most of the countries in that block incorporate disability into their constitutions and services are organised primarily to keep people in or return them to the labour force and only after that, are rehabilitation or social care services provided. However, it needs to be borne in mind that recent upheavals may well mean that old constitutional rights have disappeared along with the 'iron curtain' and the 'Berlin wall'. Similarly, as Eastern Europe opens up, evidence is becoming available that despite having constitutional rights, many disabled people experienced profound infringements to their basic human rights.

A recent estimate suggests that in the People's Republic of China, there are approximately 51 million disabled people in a population of 10 billion (Ming 1993). This suggests a prevalence of one in 20 of the population which is about half of the numbers estimated in other parts of the world. This discrepancy could be explained in a number of ways: the difficulties of providing reliable data for such a huge population; different economic and social conditions; higher or lower survival rates among disabled people and so on. The point is that, however reliable the estimates are, a substantial number of people in China are disabled.

Little is known about the welfare rights of disabled people in the People's Republic of China, though one visitor summarised the situation thus.

> There is no national social security system or network of personal social services. There are very few mobility aids, and welfare benefits are distributed from the school or workplace. If you are not in school or you are unable to work, then you remain with your family, which does not receive any specific support, or you live in a social welfare institution run by your local Bureau of Civil Affairs.
>
> (Potts 1989: 169)

The situation may be beginning to change however. Since Deng PuFang, the son of the late leader Deng Xiaou Ping, acquired a permanent spinal cord injury he is playing an active role in promoting disability issues. In 1990 the People's Congress issued a document promoting the rights of disabled people in the area of medical care and rehabilitation, welfare, education and employment. However, it seems likely that, as in most other parts of the world, Chinese disabled people have yet to see the rhetoric translated into reality (Stone 1996).

In many respects this is also the case with regard to certain sections of the disabled population in those Western countries which have introduced some form of anti-discrimination policy, In America, Australia and Canada, for example, although some issues are now being addressed – notably, those relating to environmental access – discrimination in key areas such as employment, community-based support and acute health care remain a major problem (Rioux and Bach 1994; Finkelstein 1996; Gething 1997; Rioux *et al.* 1997). Thus, underpinning our contention (Barnes and Oliver 1995; Campbell and Oliver 1996) that within a late capitalist framework, though legislation is a much needed and major step forward in the general struggle for inclusion for disabled people, 'complete barrier removal and integration into society lies in the future' (Pfeiffer 1997: 771).

Conclusion

From our review of welfare policy both here and in other parts of the world, it is clear that disabled people experience systematic deprivation and disadvantage all over the world despite the fact that substantial sums of money are being spent on welfare policies promoting inclusion. Until recently, governments have taken the view that the way to deal with this is through the provision of professional services aimed at meeting individual needs, coupled with a strategy aimed at persuading the rest of society to remove their disabling barriers and to change their restrictive environments.

Professionalised service provision within a needs-based system of welfare have added to existing forms of discrimination and have also created new forms of their own including the provision of stigmatised segregated services such as day care and the development of professional assessments and practices based on invasions of privacy as well as creating a language of paternalism which can only enhance discriminatory practices. This situation has been exacerbated by countries like Britain exporting these professionally dominated, needs-led models of welfare to parts of the developing world.

Earlier, following Davis (1996), Stone (1985) and Hahn (1985) we suggested that policy discourses played a key role in service provision because:

Discourse is about more than language. Discourse is about the interplay between language and social relationships, in which some groups are able to achieve dominance for their interests in the way in which the world is defined and acted upon. Such groups include not only dominant economic classes, but also men within patriarchy, and white people within the racism of colonial and post-colonial societies, as well as professionals in relation to service users. Language is a central aspect of discourse through which power is reproduced and communicated.

(Hugman 1991: 37)

While the discourses about disability in history and culture have been many, the modernist discourse has constructed disabled people as tragic individuals needing help and treatment and disabled people as a group needing welfare provision. Michael Ignatieff argues that this discourse of welfare provision which emphasises compassion, caring and altruism, is inappropriate when applied to citizenship for:

The language of citizenship is not properly about compassion at all, since compassion is a private virtue which cannot be legislated or enforced. The practice of citizenship is about ensuring everyone the entitlements necessary to the exercise of their liberty. As a political question, welfare is about rights, not caring, and the history of citizenship has been the struggle to make freedom real, not to tie us all in the leading strings of therapeutic good intentions.

(Ignatieff 1989: 72)

Thus, the dominant policy discourse of the late twentieth century has been essentially exclusionary, helping to ensure that disabled children are still considered to have 'special educational needs' distinct from those of non-disabled peers, that the numbers of disabled people who are unemployed increases, and that the number of disabled people living in poverty continues to rise. And this is generally the case all over the world.

However, as we discuss in more detail later, disabled people are beginning to demand rights to appropriate welfare services to meet their own self-defined needs and not to have them defined and met by others:

disabled people themselves are demanding a new emphasis on civil rights, equal opportunities and citizenship. They see institutional discrimination as the main disability they face, and are lobbying for new equal rights legislation to outlaw discrimination on the grounds of disability. The first priority is equal access to basic essentials such as an adequate income, housing, access to employment, to public transport, to education and to the ordinary facilities of everyday life.

(Doyle and Harding 1992: 72)

This is a significant shift in the discourses about disability, building on the insights of the disabled people's movement and the 'social model of disability'. Issues of discrimination and civil rights are now on the political agenda and have become part of the welfare discourse. One commentator suggests that disabled people are: 'seeking a model of welfare built not on need and philanthropy, but on equal citizenship as a means of self determination' (Coote 1992: 5).

In the terms used in this book, the word citizenship could be substituted with the word inclusion. However, the insights of the disabled people's movement and the social model of disability is discussed in some detail in Chapters 5, 6 and 7.

CHAPTER 5

Social constructions of disability and policy

Introduction

This chapter traces the ways in which our perceptions of impairment and disability have recently been transformed. We concentrate on theoretical developments within the social sciences during the twentieth century. In so doing, we show how these macro understandings have influenced professional knowledge and policy-making. The discussion centres on social constructions of disability, drawing on functionalist sociology, Weberian social theory, pluralist political approaches, gender and feminist studies, postmodernist theorising and a social oppression perspective using a 'materialist' or barriers approach. The latter is inextricably linked to the emergence and development of the disabled people's movement and is frequently referred to as the 'social model of disability'.

Normalising disability

One of the most influential social theorists to impact on social constructions of disability is the American sociologist Talcott Parsons because of his work on sickness-related behaviour (Parsons 1951). Parsons' approach is responsible for two distinct but interdependent approaches which have implicitly or explicitly influenced all subsequent analyses. They are the relevance of the 'sick role' and its link with social deviance, and the notion of health as adaptation (Bury 1982; Oliver 1996).

Each of these approaches rests on Western notions of individuality and health; the responsibility for recovery rests with the disabled person. They are dependent on 'rehabilitation' professionals for at least two important functions: first, the initiation of rehabilitation programmes designed to return them to 'normality', and second, assistance in the psychological accommodation of a 'disabled' identity. Finally, a major factor explaining the continued relevance of functionalist theory is its professional expediency, both at the individual and at the structural levels. If individuals fail to achieve the anticipated professionally determined rehabilitation goals, then this failure can be explained with reference to the disabled person's perceived inadequacy: whether it be physically or intellectually based or both.

At the structural level, functionalism supports the continued dominance of professionally controlled welfare services. The professional 'expert' is exonerated from responsibility for any failures in welfare provision, professional integrity remains intact, traditional wisdom and values are not questioned, and the existing social order remains unchallenged (Barnes 1990).

A variant of functionalism is that of normalisation theory. Over the last decade or so the 'normalisation' principle has become particularly influential in the field of disability, especially with reference to people with intellectual impairments or 'learning difficulties'. It is widely associated with the Canadian theorist, Wolf Wolfensberger, who redefined it as a 'meta theory' or 'meta system' with many corollaries that effect not only the most clinical and direct services, but also the structural and systemic aspects of service systems (Wolfensberger 1980: 7).

A summary of Wolfensberger's formulation involves first, the adoption of culturally valued mechanisms to enable people to lead culturally valued lives; second, the use of culturally normative means to provide life conditions which are as good as those of the average citizen; third, the enhancement of the behaviour, appearance, experience and status of the devalued person; and fourth, the use of culturally normative means to support behaviour, appearance, experience and status which are themselves culturally normative (Chappell 1992: 32). Over the last two decades the normalisation principle has been championed by many theorists, policy-makers and practitioners alike, particularly in Western societies such as America, Australia, Britain and Canada. For Wolfensberger, normalisation is a principle which can be applied to all disabled people and, indeed, everyone who is perceived as deviant. Throughout, assumptions about the 'quality' of life and/or services are based on the normalisation principle (Oliver 1994: 14).

Normalisation, therefore, is a theory of services not of disability. Moreover, as services are controlled by professionals, it enables them to retain a key role in their delivery and debates about quality. Thus, it has successfully facilitated their adaptation to deinstitutionalisation and the newer community-based provision and practices. As with Parsons' functionalist analysis, discussed earlier, 'normalisation' does not challenge the legitimacy of the professional role in the lives of disabled people, but legitimates it and its continued authority.

In common with other functionalist approaches, Wolfensberger's attempt to deconstruct the process of deviance creation simply reproduces discriminatory norms and values by failing to address the cultural and economic forces which precipitate them. His use of the concept of 'culturally valued roles' for individuals with impairments, implicitly if not explicitly, undermines and devalues the social contribution and unique characteristics of those who do not appear to conform to such stereotypes. The whole focus of this approach is on changing disabled people to make them more like 'normal' people. Practitioners of normalisation seek to 'enhance' the lives of disabled people without seriously addressing the disabling society in which they live out their lives. In this way, the process of 'normalising' people and services constructs and maintains the 'normal/abnormal dichotomy' (Oliver 1994: 12).

The crucial problem is that disabled people, regardless of the type and/or the severity of impairment, cannot be considered an homogeneous group which can be accommodated easily within a society which takes little or no account of their individual and/or collective needs. As with the population as a whole, disabled people are characterised by difference rather than normality: differences in terms of gender, minority ethnic background, sexual orientation, age, abilities, religious beliefs, wealth, access to work and so on. Clearly, their situation cannot be understood or, indeed, transformed by any theory or policy which is based on conventional notions of normality and the existence of a single set of culturally dominant values.

Rationalisating and bureaucratisating disability

Using the theories of the German nineteenth-century sociologist Max Weber (1948), albeit unacknowledged, the American political scientist Deborah A. Stone (1985) argues that capitalist development is accompanied by a process of intensifying rationalisation and bureaucratisation and that constructions of disability play a key role in the development of social policy. Through a detailed historical account of social policy developments in America, Britain and Germany she asserts that all societies function through a complex system of commodity production and distribution; the principal means of allocation is work. But because not everyone is able or willing to work, a 'distributive dilemma' arises about how to allocate resources on the very different principles of work and need.

The problem is resolved through the development of the concept 'disability': a boundary category through which people are allocated either to the work-based or to the needs-based system of commodity distribution. For Stone, the increasing specialisation of both categorisation and provision is the outcome of the increased rationalisation and bureaucratisation of the Western world. Unlike the functionalist accounts discussed above, this approach is more questioning of professionally dominated and controlled welfare services.

Thus, the 'social construction of disability' is the result of the state's need to control access to the state-sponsored welfare system and the inevitable accumulation of power by those charged with the responsibility for allocation: the medical, rehabilitation and legal professions. The escalating cost of this seemingly ever-expanding and increasingly rigid needs-based system will bring about an eventual system breakdown. This, Stone suggests, can only be resolved by a retreat from state-sponsored welfarism, and a re-emphasis on individual responsibility and prevention (Stone 1985).

This line of argument is extended further by Wolf Wolfensberger (1989), who seems unaware of the contradictions with his other arguments on normalisation. In a short but incisive analysis of the recent experience of Western societies, Wolfensberger argues that the social construction of disability and dependence is a latent function of the unprecedented growth of 'human service industries': examples include the medical, rehabilitation and legal professions in the post-1945 period.

Although these agencies have manifest or stated purposes or functions, it is the latent or unacknowledged functions which are the most powerful. These are the covert functions of human services that are achieved in subtle and indirect ways. Wolfensberger maintains that in a 'post primary production economy', where manufacturing is no longer the main economic activity, human service industries have become more important. Their unspecified function is to create and sustain large numbers of seemingly dependent and, therefore, devalued people in order to secure employment for others. This is in marked contrast to their stated function which is to rehabilitate such people back into the community (Wolfensberger 1989).

A more comprehensive analysis is provided by an American sociologist Gary Albrecht (1992). He argues that 'disability' is produced by 'the disability business'. Drawing on anthropological and historical material, Albrecht shows how the kind of society in which people live produces certain types of disease, impairment and disability. Utilising what he terms an 'ecological model', he traces the ways in which the physical, biophysical and cultural environments interact to produce particular biophysical conditions and social responses to impairment. Hence, in modern America, the combination of industrialisation, the subsequent growth of the human service sector, and the more recent politicisation of 'disability rights' by the American disabled people's movement have transformed 'disability' and 'rehabilitation' into a multi-million dollar enterprise. This poses particular economic and social problems for the future, both for the disabled community and for society as a whole. His solution is the further development of a 'pluralist political economy of rehabilitation', based on the current American system, in which: 'persons with disabilities [*sic*] must either accept the socially constructed definitions laid on them or fight for a *personal* [emphasis added] redefinition' (Albrecht 1992: 375).

Undoubtedly, each of the above represents, to varying degrees, an alternative to conventional individualistic interpretations of disability, yet they each fail to address some of the key structural factors precipitating their application. Consequently, disabled people tend to be treated as an abstract, somehow distinct from the rest of the human race, and the crucial question of causality is fudged rather than clarified. For example, Albrecht (1992: 35) states that:

disability is constituted both by impairments and the disabling environment. The concept of disabling environments, however, forces us to acknowledge that disabilities are physically based but socially constructed. Societies, then, produce disabilities differently from impairments.

Equally important is the fact that the central value system, or 'ideological cornerstones', on which Western society rests goes unchallenged. Certainly, in a later paper (1994) Wolfensberger addresses what he terms 'modernistic values' but these are the direct outcome of the 'collapse of Western society' in the latter half of the twentieth century. Albrecht's notion of the 'cultural environment' encompasses abstract concepts like the 'human populations', 'economy', 'means of production', 'social organisation' and 'ideologies'; his discussion of the latter is limited to half a page. He concedes that issues like poverty, race, ethnicity, gender and age are significant factors in the construction and production of disability, but the theoretical and cultural implications of these insights are never fully explored.

In policy terms, the outcome for disabled people is rather depressing. While these theorists, to different degrees, acknowledge the role of individuals as well as that of structure in that they recognise the existence of disability politics, they do not see disabled people as increasingly playing a key role in shaping both policy and practice. Instead, disabled people are seen as passive victims of rationalising and bureaucratising structural forces.

Disability as politics

A growing concern over the increasing professionalisation and politicisation of disability prompted an American political scientist Harlan Hahn (1986) to reconceptualise a 'new minority group' model of disability which challenged other disability paradigms. Focusing primarily on what he terms the 'lack of conceptual clarity' in American social policy for disabled people, Hahn shows how this 'socio/political' approach has evolved from what he considers to be its predecessors: the medical and the economic variants.

Referring to the growing challenge to medical and economic definitions of disability by the burgeoning disabled people's movement, Hahn subsequently identifies what he terms a 'new socio/political' approach to disability. Based firmly in 'sociological theories' of 'stigmatisation' and 'labelling', he suggests that the distinguishing features of disabled people – physical and behavioural characteristics, which set them apart from the rest of American society, their growing collective awareness, together with their differential treatment – necessitates their redefinition as a 'minority group' in common with ethnic, racial and other oppressed minorities. This, he maintains, provides the basis for an emphasis on legal and civil rights in recognition of the fact that improvements to the status of people with impairments 'requires changes primarily to the external environment rather than to their physical or economic skills' (Hahn 1986: 132).

In contrast to previous definitions which reflect professional evaluations, Hahn contends that this new perspective seeks to embody the social meaning of disability derived from the lived experience of disabled men and women. Such a perspective is based on an explicit recognition that 'discriminatory attitudes', rather than functional impairments, lie at the heart of the problem. He also acknowledges that 'in a fundamental sense, the ultimate origins of the problems facing disabled citizens probably can be traced to the nature of economic systems such as capitalism' (Hahn 1986: 133).

While this work does bring individual experiences into the explanation it is located within the context of pluralist political theorising. The disabled people's movement is seen almost exclusively in terms of advocacy, self-help and civil rights struggles. Policy changes will occur to the extent that disabled people can use the civil rights'framework to ensure their own, individual inclusion into capitalist America, as it is. Little mention is given to the significance of the more recent collective approaches, sometimes referred to as 'new social movements' (Oliver 1996), and the disabled people's movement in particular and the real challenge they pose to the production of disability: its cultural representations and the possible transformation of the concept of disability from a commodity to a political weapon. This analysis, which we return to later, insists that the route to inclusion is through complete social transformation and not simply in terms of the extension of the idea of civil rights to disabled people.

Gendered disability

One of the earliest attempts to address the relationship between gender and disability is Jo Campling's *Better Lives for Disabled Women* (1979), later followed by her *Images of Ourselves: Women with Disabilities Talking* (1981). Although Campling considered herself 'able bodied' in the early 1980s, she grew up in a 'disabled family' – her mother contracted polio at the age of three. As a consequence she has a lifetime's experience of disability. Hence, these books provide vivid first-hand accounts of the panoply of ways in which gender impacts on the experience of living with impairment. Indeed, Campling makes no attempt to locate these phenomena within a social context, preferring to let the essays speak for themselves.

For the American theorists Michelle Fine and Adrianne Asch (1985), however, the general failure to address the oppression of disabled women can be explained with reference to the dominance of male values in Western society. They suggest that it is this value system which encourages disabled men to oppose the stigma associated with impairment and enables them to aspire to typical male roles. In contrast, disabled women do not have a comparable option. They are 'perceived as inadequate for economically productive roles (traditionally considered appropriate for males) and for the nurturant, reproductive roles considered appropriate for women' (Fine and Asch 1985: 6). They maintain that the lack of approved social roles for disabled women is derived from a variety of confounding forces. Moreover, like racial or minority ethnic women, they experience a significant disadvantage in relation to their relevant 'single minority reference groups': that is, disabled men and non-disabled women. This is a 'double' disadvantage because women with impairments fare far worse than both groups 'economically, socially and psychologically'. Fine and Asch assert that the extent of disabled women's oppression is not a natural occurrence but the outcome of structural forces: 'The combined forces of a hostile economy, a discriminating society and a negative self-image contribute to a systematic rolelessness for disabled women' (Fine and Asch 1985: 9).

Subsequent studies in Britain (Morris 1989; Lonsdale 1990) provided empirical data on the degree of oppression encountered by disabled women on account of gender. Similar themes are central to Jenny Morris' later work (1991) where she provides a broadly feminist perspective on the experience of disablement, a critique of earlier 'male dominated socio-logical' accounts of disability, and an expression and celebration of the individual and collective strength gained from her involvement with other disabled people in the disabled people's movement.

For Morris, prejudice is all-embracing, takes a variety of forms, ranging from pity to hatred, and is continuous. Consequently, it is not simply environmental and social barriers that preclude disabled people from community life but also 'the knowledge that each entry into the public world will be dominated by stares, by condescension, by pity, and by hostility' (Morris 1991: 25). This places enormous pressure on disabled people to conform to 'non-disabled' ideals and constitutes the first and foremost obstacle to disabled people's individual and collective empowerment.

Morris is particularly concerned about the nature and uncertainty of current welfare systems for disabled people and this brings her into conflict with established feminist perspectives. In conjunction with the disabled people's movement, she is critical of present day 'community care' policies which reinforce dependence and passivity (Morris 1993). In partial alliance with feminism, she is critical of current policies which rely on traditional assumptions that women will act as unpaid 'carers' for disabled and dependent family members.

Because the 'burden of care' falls disproportionately on women, non-disabled feminists such as Gillian Dalley (1988), for example, have called for a more 'collectivist' approach which includes the greater use of residential type services, albeit not on the old large-scale institution-type model. While not disagreeing with notions of mutual support, Morris points out that such arguments are a further indication of feminism's failure to address the experience of disability and to challenge stereo-types of dependency:

By taking the need for care for granted and by assuming the dependency of older and disabled people, feminist research and carers as a pressure group have not only failed to address the interests of older and disabled people but they have, unwittingly, colluded with both the creation of dependency and the state's reluctance to tackle the social and economic factors which disable people. In so doing they have failed to challenge either the poverty of older and disabled people, or the discrimination and social prejudice which characterises their interactions with individuals and social institutions.

(Morris 1993: 49)

Jenny Morris' work is important because by bringing a uniquely feminist perspective to the analysis of disability she focuses on a number of key issues in the lives of disabled women which have significant implications for the disabled community as a whole, and which hitherto had been ignored or undervalued by the majority of disability theorists. These include selective abortion, genetic screening, euthanasia and cultural representations of impairment and disabled people.

In policy terms, her solutions to the ways in which welfare structures reinforce discrimination and social prejudice are to build on the insights of the disabled people's movement and their approach to 'independent living', discussed in detail in Chapter 7. Specifically in respect of gender, she insists it has to be recognised that informal carers only exist as an oppressed social group because of the social, economic and political oppression of disabled people. The solution, therefore, is the eradication of the oppression of disabled people.

Disability and difference

Within sociology and social policy, postmodernism is a concept generally linked to recent developments in Western capitalist societies, and correlates with what Wolfensberger (1989) termed the shift from a primary to a post-primary production economy. It is associated with the decline of traditional 'Fordist' type methods of mass production and marketing by big industrial companies employing large semi-skilled workforces producing goods for mass markets, and their replacement by burgeoning 'Post-Fordist' economic systems. These are usually small-scale operations utilising specialist 'batch' production techniques employing a smaller multiskilled and flexible workforce. Markets are said to be segmented or pluralist in nature, since not everyone wants the same thing.

Late capitalist or 'postmodern' society is characterised by a fragmented and complex social structure in which social class has declined in importance; other sources of social differentiation include gender, ethnicity, sexuality and disability. Centralised 'big government' and traditional large political organisations such as trade unions are said to be in retreat because of the intensified competitiveness of the market, the subsequent promotion of the importance of self-reliance, private enterprise, and the privatisation of the welfare state.

For many postmodernists, cultural factors lie at the heart of these developments. These include the growing importance of the culture industries and their impact on everyday life, and the construction of individual and collective identities through self-determination and choice rather than by traditional ascription (Featherstone *et al.* 1991). They view both the idea and practice of universalist welfare states as part of the failure of modernity, eschewing the possibilities of such large-scale projects which inevitably turn out to be controlling rather than liberating.

The American writer Helen Liggett (1988) adopts a 'postmodernist' perspective to focus attention on the way in which the 'disabled subject' is produced by the discursive practices of American social policy. She sees the 'politics of disability' in terms of various attempts to influence government policy to reduce the negative effects of impairment. But, following the French philosopher Michel Foucault's (1977) efforts to link interpretation, truth and politics, she adopts what she calls an interpretative approach.

As a consequence she seeks to address the problematic nature of 'interpretative contexts'. Her approach, she maintains, differs from previous theoretical approaches. These include the positivist perspective which connects truth to objects outside of language and the phenomenological position as it links truth to the consciousness of 'individual knowers' and their use of language. Instead of preceding language, the existence of subjects and objects are inseparable from its use. Consequently, the true nature or 'epistemology' of 'objects' like disability is negotiable because it is embedded in the 'commerce of everyday life'. She cites Deborah Stone's (1985) analysis of the emergence of the disability category (discussed earlier) as an example of this type of perspective. Therefore, disability, as a social construct, is an available identity within particular societal conditions.

Utilising Foucault's concepts of the 'carceral network' and the 'normalising society' she explains the production and control of disabled people in modern society as the same 'discursive practices' which manage criminality and madness. She suggests that the 'normalising' society is inescapable and that 'normal' identities are just as much products of the 'discipline' of everyday life as are deviant ones. The 'normalising society' is a structure of dominance based on relations of force involving all society's members.

For Liggett, the Foucauldian distinction between normal and deviant is analogous to the division between non-disabled and disabled people. Consequently, all previous attempts to rationalise disability policy are doomed to failure because they produce solutions which contribute to the further development of the disciplinary society. On the other hand, they are successful if their primary aim is to discipline and control the disabled population. She points out that pluralist political theorists committed to the empowerment of disabled people through the minority group approach encourage disabled people to participate in their own administration and control. Although she concedes that the minority group approach has certain advantages in that it gives disabled people a legitimate voice within capitalist society and, therefore, the opportunity to change some of the 'agents of domination', it is, nonetheless, a double-edged sword.

For Liggett this dilemma might be resolved by first, the production of a detailed 'genealogy' or interpretative account of disability which investigates and evaluates the shifting social practices which constitute and administer disability in the normalising society; and second, by the development of alternative political strategies. A key aspect of the 'genealogy' of disability would address the question of how disability relates to Foucault's notion that disciplinary power produces subjects by operating 'directly on the bodies'. In terms of political strategies, these would involve a 'reflective' undertaking in which both the costs and benefits of accepting or rejecting disabled identities are weighed in each individual situation (Liggett 1988: 272).

The problem about Liggett's recipe for political action is that such strategies could easily resemble 'special pleading' and undermine the tactics that disabled people have adopted for themselves (Oliver and Zarb 1989: 225). These include the personal and public affirmation of a 'disabled identity', and the demand that they be accepted by and integrated into society as they are: namely, as people with impairments.

The politics of disability seen from the 'new social movement' perspective (Oliver 1990; Campbell and Oliver 1996) entails the acceptance of collective action as a means to social transformation and a rejection of the notion of the impaired body in need of eradication or cure. While not all would accept the usefulness of this analysis (Shakespeare 1993; Fagan and Lee 1997), about which more will be said later, the fact remains that, however theorised, the action of disabled people is increasingly having a significant impact on social policy and welfare states.

Disability as social oppression

A materialist theory of disability was originally advanced by the clinical psychologist, disability activist and founder member of the Union of the Physically Impaired Against Segregation (UPIAS) Vic Finkelstein (1980) when he argued that disability was the direct result of the development of Western industrial society. Using a conventional materialist framework, Finkelstein divided history into three distinct sequential phases. The first, Phase One, broadly corresponds to the feudal period before European industrialisation. Here economic activity consisted primarily of agrarian or cottage-based industries: a 'mode of production', he maintains, which did not preclude people with perceived impairments from participation.

But in Phase Two, round about the nineteenth century, when industrialisation took hold, people with impairments were excluded from employment on the grounds that they were unable to keep pace with the new factory-based work system. Hence, they were segregated from the mainstream of economic and social activity into a variety of residential institutions. Finkelstein's third phase, which he maintains is only just beginning, will see the eventual liberation of disabled people from such oppression through the development and use of technology, and their working together with helpers and allies toward commonly held goals.

In Phase One, people with impairments were dispersed throughout the community; but in Phase Two, because of the emergence of large-scale industry with production lines geared to 'able bodied norms' and 'hospital based medicine' (p. 10), they were separated from their social origins into a clearly defined, devalued group. Phase Three will witness the end of the paradox as disability will be recognised as social restriction only.

In the decade following the publication of Finkelstein's schema, the notion of disability as social oppression was used extensively by disabled writers and activists to explore their own experiences of prejudice and discrimination (Sutherland 1981). The disabled sociologist Paul Abberley (1987) called for a more comprehensive theoretical approach, suggesting that a theory of disability as social oppression must also 'argue that these disadvantages [that disabled people experience] are dialectically related to an ideology or group of ideologies which justify and perpetuate this situation' (Abberley 1987: 7). This was forthcoming with the publication of *The Politics of Disablement* (Oliver 1990). This book attempts to provide a comprehensive materialist account of the creation of disability placing 'ideology' at the centre of the argument. Here, ideology refers to a set of values and beliefs distinct from theology or metaphysics but rooted in notions of post-enlightenment rationality which underpins social policies and practices including those in the work place, medical intervention, welfare services, and the leisure and culture industries. Hence, the material and social disadvantages associated with impairment are related to the core ideology of individualism, and the peripheral ideologies of medicalisation and rehabilitation, all of which emerged within the context of capitalist development.

Anthropological evidence is also provided to show that these disadvantages are not apparent in all societies, demonstrating that this group of ideologies are neither natural nor inevitable. Moreover, it is the system as a whole which benefits since, economically, disabled people form part of a 'reserve army of labour' and, ideologically, they 'serve as a warning to those unable or unwilling to work' (Oliver 1990: 70). In sum, economic development, the changing nature of ideas, and the need to maintain order during industrialisation influenced social responses to and, therefore, the experience of impairment and disability. The rise of the institution as a means of both social provision and control, coupled with the individualisation and medicalisation of 'social problems' in the eighteenth and nineteenth centuries, facilitated the exclusion of disabled people from mainstream capitalist society.

Unlike the approaches previously discussed, these accounts suggest that the basis of disabled people's oppression is linked to the material and ideological changes associated with capitalist development. This has far-reaching implications in social policy terms both for disabled people and for society as a whole. The welfare state, while being severely implicated in the oppression of disabled people, has also been responsible for providing services and support to allow some disabled people at least, to rattle the chains of this oppression.

Materialist theories of welfare, whether deriving originally from the work of Karl Marx (1970) or explicitly in respect of disability from the work of Vic Finkelstein, may ultimately rely on Utopian notions of social transformation to resolve the oppression of disabled people. But that does not mean that they do not provide a meaningful basis for social change in the here and now. As we shall see in subsequent chapters, coupled explicitly to new social movement theory, they see current struggles for inclusion, including inclusionary welfare practices through the promotion of independent living, as steps on the long and difficult road to ultimate liberation.

Conclusion

In this chapter we have looked at the various ways disability has been theorised and constructed, and we have suggested that understanding these processes is essential in providing appropriate welfare services and practices. We have shown that theorising about the experiences of both impairment and disability within the context of the social sciences has spanned the latter half of the twentieth century. It is clear from this analysis that the bulk of this work, particularly that produced by professional academics, has tended to adhere, at least implicitly if not explicitly, to traditional wisdom and policy solutions. As a consequence, although, theoretically, the distinction between the biological and the social has become increasingly blurred, particularly in some of the more 'progressive' literature, the emphasis, in social policy terms, remains on the former, although increasingly such theorising is being challenged.

In the next chapter we examine other social constructions of disability. These include the cultural representations of impairment and disability in the mass media and their links with the construction of a conventional disabled or devalued identity, as well as those developed by disabled people themselves in attempting to construct their own individual and collective identity.

CHAPTER 6

Socially constructing a disabled identity

Introduction

Previous chapters have shown how over the latter half of the twentieth century our understanding of disability is slowly but surely being transformed. Here we consider the impact of this phenomenon from the perspective of disabled people: in particular, the redefinition of self and a recognition that the personal is political. However, since the re-evaluation of disability is only now beginning to make a significant impact on the way disability is being constructed in popular culture and the media, we suggest that the role of self-help, social and political organisation, and the emergence of a disability culture are key aspects of this process.

We begin, therefore, with a brief overview of media representations of disability and disabled people. The discussion then turns to the process of socialisation and the acquisition of a conventional 'disabled' or dependent identity. The following section examines the process of re-evaluation of self by disabled people themselves through the process of their own self-organisation. Finally, we consider the challenges to traditional disability imagery that this personal and collective liberation has produced in terms of the newly emergent disability culture. All this will be located within the context of welfare provision and we suggest that these changing constructions are beginning to have an impact on social policy.

Popular culture, media and disability

The oppression of people with impairments has been a constant feature of Western cultural development throughout recorded history. Perhaps unsurprisingly then negative cultural stereotypes and assumptions about both impairment and disability predominate within all aspects of the media, including the cinema, television, literature, newspapers and the advertising industry. Moreover, there is a growing consensus among the general public and media theorists that cultural imagery plays an important role in the process of attitude and identity formation (Inglis 1991; Broadcasting Standards Council 1994; Ang 1996; Eldridge *et al.* 1997).

Recent work on audience reactions to media coverage of AIDS by Jenny Kitzinger, for example, shows that there are widespread similarities in the way AIDS was covered in the media and how it was interpreted and understood by media audiences. The audience-reception work was based on discussions with 52 different focus groups. The respondents discussed their beliefs at length, talked about their sources of information, described their changing perceptions of the problems associated with HIV and AIDS, and wrote their own scripts for news broadcasts about the AIDS 'epidemic'.

'Factual' reporting on the radio, television and in newspapers provided people with facts and figures; it familiarised them with a particular vocabulary relative to HIV and AIDS and it introduced a new set of images. Kitzinger's analyses highlight the ways in which different elements of media coverage influence public opinion and how ignorance and misunderstandings are encouraged and reproduced by particular terminology and imagery (Kitzinger 1993, 1995). While there are no comparable studies dealing directly with audience responses to media coverage of impairment and disability, it is highly likely that a similar analysis would provide similar results.

Nonetheless, there is little doubt among disabled people and their organisations that much of the responsibility for the public image of disability lies with the media. Paul Hunt expressed the views of many when he wrote: 'We are tired of being statistics, cases, wonderfully courageous examples to the world [or] pitiable objects to stimulate funding' (Hunt 1966: x).

Indeed, one of the first examples of work focusing specifically on cultural stereotypes of disabled people is Louis Battye's 'Chatterley Syndrome' which appeared in Hunt's (1966) collection *Stigma*. Here Battye shows how in the novel *Lady Chatterley's Lover*, D. H. Lawrence perpetuates the age-old myth that disabled men are incapable of sexual activity. Now regarded as a classic of twentieth-century literature, it is a tale of a heterosexual affair between Lady Chatterley and the non-disabled gamekeeper, Meadows. The affair takes place because Lord Chatterley is represented as sexually impotent due to an impairment acquired in the First World War.

Moving from the particular to the general, a number of writers have identified several commonly occurring stereotypes of disabled people in popular culture and the media (Biklen and Bogdana 1977; Rieser and Mason 1992). Subsequently, several reviews appeared, both in America and in the UK, documenting the extent of disabling imagery in films, television, literature, the press and the advertising industry; notably, in charity advertising (Fiedler 1981; Gartner and Joe 1987; Wertheimer 1988; Scott Parker 1989; Barnes 1992; Cumberbatch and Negrine 1992; Hevey 1992; Hafferty and Foster 1994; Shakespeare 1994; Norden 1994; Garland-Thompson 1997). Of particular concern are the ways in which these images permeate media aimed specifically at children (Quicke 1985; Rieser 1992; Davidson *et al.* 1994).

Further, while there is evidence that some elements within the media are beginning to address the issues raised by these studies, on the whole,

media representations of disabled people remain unequivocally negative. The link between impairment and all that is socially unacceptable
is constantly reproduced in a variety of forms, particularly in fictional
representations. Drawing on the cultural stereotypes of earlier 'less en-
lightened' times, disabled characters regularly appear in crime and thriller
films either as criminals, monsters, or as people who are powerless and
pathetic in order to evoke fear, pity and sympathy. Recent well-known
examples include the principal villains in the Batman films: namely, the
Joker, Penguin and Two Face, and Quasimodo in the 1995 cartoon
remake of the *Hunchback of Notre Dame* by the Walt Disney studio.

Alternatively, films such as *Born on the Fourth of July* (1989) or
Tommy (1975) are examples of films which present disabled characters
as superhuman, overcoming immense personal tragedy. The first is a
story about a Vietnam veteran responding to the onset of impairment
caused by a war injury. The second is a rock opera about a 'deaf, dumb
and blind kid' who is unbeatable on pinball machines. There are fewer
portrayals of disabled women in films but when they do appear it is
usually as helpless victims. Examples include Hollywood classics such
as *Whatever Happened to Baby Jane* (1962) and *Wait until Dark* (1967).
In the former a wheelchair user, Joan Crawford, is physically and verb-
ally abused by her murderous sister, Bette Davis. In the latter, Audrey
Hepburn, who plays a blind woman, is terrorised by a gang of male
thugs looking for drugs. These films and countless others with similar
themes are regularly repeated on television: the most popular form of
home entertainment.

All these stereotypical constructions of disabled people as passive
and dependent reinforce the ideology underpinning welfare service
provision. Disabled people's apparent passivity suggests that they need
professional advocates to articulate their interests and their dependency
means that they require services that take care of them. Further, stereotypical constructions of disabled people as having 'something wrong
with them' based on reports of impairment, specific medical treatments
and triumph-over-tragedy stories continue to dominate the coverage of
disability issues on television factual programming such as documen-
taries and news broadcasts. This undervalues disabled people's contribution to society and reinforces the misguided assumption that all disabled
people have a medical 'problem' which prevents them from participating
in the mainstream economic and social life of the community.

These negative constructions are further re-enforced by the advertising industry. First, disabled characters are generally absent from mainstream advertising. Besides rendering disabled people invisible, this
practice undermines their role in the economy as consumers. Second,
some advertisers, notably, charities, present a particularly distorted view
of the experience of impairment to raise money, recruit volunteers and
publicise their activities. Repeatedly, heart-rending images and messages depicting tragedy, loss or bravery are used to ensure continued
public and, increasingly, government support. This form of exploitation
is a major issue for growing numbers of disabled people.

The disabled photographer David Hevey summarises the views of many in the following statement:

It [charity advertising] represents the highest public validation of the isolation of disabled people. It presents a solution to the 'problem' of disablement by a disguised blaming of the victim. It fails to provide a solution because it is itself the problem. But what is missing from charity advertising is the centre of this grand solution – the separating out of impairment from the disablement, the medical view from the social view.

The dominant form of impairment imagery, that of charity advertising, cannot demonstrate the struggle because the very essence of charities is to obstruct the making of the link.

(Hevey 1992: 51)

There is often an explicit link between these opportunistic charitable constructions and welfare provision in that many of the charities responsible are major service providers in the voluntary sector of the welfare state. Hence, there is a double pay-off to the constructions they promote: not only do they maximise income but they legitimate the continued provision of passivity and dependency, creating segregated provision such as residential homes, day centres and segregated special schools.

Constructing individual disabled identities

Clearly, within Western society to have an impairment is 'abnormal' and something to be avoided at all costs. Men and women with congenital impairments are, implicitly if not explicitly, dissuaded from parenting children with similar conditions. Pregnant women 'at risk' of giving birth to a 'handicapped fetus' – the medical euphemism for an unborn disabled child – are encouraged to have abortions. Living with impairment is generally associated with poverty, social isolation and stigmatisation or second-class citizenship. To become 'disabled' is to be assigned a new identity indicating membership of a separate tribe or species. To be born with an impairment is to have this identity assigned from the moment of discovery and diagnosis. Both involve a social learning process in which the nuances and meanings of this identity have to be assimilated or addressed.

In short, we learn the social norms, cultural expectations and shared standards of behaviour of society through the process of socialisation. Primary socialisation relates to the experience of childhood. It is generally regarded as the most important, and often takes place within the family. Hence, besides the communications media and families, other important agencies of socialisation include the education system, work – occupational groupings and work experience – and various elements in the leisure industry: sport for example. Through interactions with 'significant others' – parents, siblings, peers and, particularly in the case of disabled people, professionals – we learn the roles we are expected to perform both as children and as adults. Socialisation is not confined to childhood but continues throughout adulthood.

Perceptions of self are, therefore, derived through the continuous process of social interaction. We come to know who we are and how we are perceived as individuals through our interaction with other people. Hence, we assemble a concept of self based on how we imagine others see us. Our sense of identity is constructed on the basis of other people's definitions. For example, how a child with a congenital impairment adapts to societal perceptions of disability will, initially at least, be greatly influenced by interactions within the family (Beazley and Moore 1995; Lewis 1995).

This social learning process for people with devalued identities was described in detail by the Canadian social psychologist Erving Goffman (1968). His analysis of the 'moral career', or changes in self-perception, of socially stigmatised individuals suggests that the acquisition of the devalued identity is a two-stage learning process. The first stage relates to learning the values and beliefs of mainstream society and the general idea of what it would be like to be viewed abnormally. The second stage begins when the disabled individual learns that they are viewed in this way, and then discovers the consequences of this perception. The timing and interplay of these two stages are crucial, Goffman notes, as they influence an individual's ability to respond to their particular circumstances.

When applied to people with perceived impairments Goffman conceptualised this process in four ways. The first concerns people with congenital conditions and involves individuals being socialised into accepting their disadvantaged circumstances even while they are learning and incorporating the standards against which they fall short. The majority of disabled children grow up in households and communities where there are no other disabled people. Consequently, unlike other oppressed groups such as women and Black people, for example, they do not have strong supportive role models with which to identify. Indeed, several factors, including the actions of well-meaning but ill-informed parents, protracted professional intervention, lengthy periods of hospitalisation, segregated special education, and a largely inaccessible physical environment combine to ensure that many disabled children grow up apparently accepting the many economic and social deprivations associated with a conventional 'disabled identity' (Barnes 1990).

This is often accompanied and exacerbated by an extreme form of self-depreciation or 'internal oppression', the consequences of which are extremely difficult to overcome. The following statement from Micheline Mason, a disabled mother and activist, sums up the situation well:

Once oppression has been internalised, little force is needed to keep us submissive. We harbour inside ourselves the pain and the memories, the fears and the confusions, the negative and the low expectations, turning them into weapons with which to injure ourselves every day of our lives.

(Mason 1992: 27)

Goffman's second route also relates to people impaired from birth but involves individuals being shielded by institutions such as the family or special schools until they enter the wider community either at school, or later during adolescence. Several studies suggest that disabled young people are apparently unaware of the consequences of living with perceived impairment until they begin to look for work or try to participate in mainstream leisure activities. As a consequence, self-depreciation and low self-esteem are particularly high among disabled young people during their teenage years and early twenties (Anderson *et al.* 1982; Thomas *et al.* 1989; Barnes 1990; Hirst and Baldwin 1995).

The third variant refers to people with acquired impairments, and concerns the re-evaluation of self following the ascription of a disabled identity. Newly disabled people are said to 'grieve' and 'mourn' for recently lost abilities. But besides the consequences of impairment, this is often caused by the realisation that becoming disabled usually means the exclusion from previously taken-for-granted everyday activities. The ensuing sense of despair can be almost overwhelming, as the following testimony from a disabled woman, Maggie Hines, illustrates:

I thought, 'this is it, they're shutting me right out just because I'm disabled' . . . I then began to realise that things were not as accessible to disabled people as they were to able-bodied people. I started getting pretty depressed after that because I knew things were going to be pretty hard . . . I started realising that I didn't have much hope, there wasn't going to be a job. I had nowhere to go and I just wondered 'Well what sort of future is there at all?'

(cited in Campbell and Oliver 1996: 106)

Goffman's fourth model concerns individuals socialised into an alien culture, who are confronted with the problem of self-reappraisal after learning that their adopted norms and values are not viewed as appropriate by those around them or, indeed, by themselves (Goffman 1968). Although for Goffman this variant was not really applicable to people with perceived impairments, in many ways it encapsulates the perspective of all disabled people struggling to retain a sense of self-worth in a culture increasingly geared to the myth of non-disabled normality.

Moreover, because coming to terms with the ascription of a conventional disabled identity can be an emotionally tortuous process, many disabled people go through a period of denial. This refers to the situation in which a disabled person identifies with the non-disabled world and tries to minimise or disregard the impact of their impairment during the course of their daily lives. Denial can take many forms. For example, people with hidden impairments such as epilepsy or diabetes are sometimes able to conceal their condition and pass as 'normal' (Goffman 1968). But passing as normal generally involves considerable tensions and difficulties managing relevant information and social interaction, the consequences of which are often a profound sense of social isolation. The following statement from Eddy, a man with a congenital physical and visible impairment, illustrates the point well:

I was normal like everybody else and I had the opinion that I was better than disabled people, and I wasn't disabled, but I couldn't pass a full-length mirror and I had very low self-esteem as a disabled person. I just couldn't see that I was disabled. I knew I was but I just couldn't accept it.

(cited in Shakespeare 1996: 50)

Another form of denial is where the disabled person seeks to overcome the consequences of impairment at any price. Often a strategy associated with traditional 'masculine' expectations, it involves a refusal to submit to reality, and an attempt to regain or retain what is perceived as a 'normal' identity through intense competitive activity such as sport or certain types of employment (Shakespeare 1996).

While these and other strategies may demonstrate the human capacity for adaptation, they each involve a degree of denial or failure and an acceptance of external disempowering agendas. Moreover, they each represent a short-term or compromise solution which is ultimately fragile and, therefore, brings with it risks in terms of psychological stability and social wellbeing. As the disabled writer Tom Shakespeare notes: 'The disabled person is trapped in a prison not of their own devising, and cannot escape except through strategies which are ultimately self-defeating' (Shakespeare 1996: 101).

Conversely, it should be remembered that in an increasingly harsh world a conventional disabled identity has particular attractions. This is particularly the case for people who are located at the foot of the economic and social system, and already subject to multiple deprivation. Indeed, in the absence of other socially sanctioned identities the 'professional cripple role' enables disabled individuals to interact successfully with professionals and offers the 'benefits of sympathy and concern' from others. Consequently acceptance and assimilation takes precedence over self-realisation.

The person with an impairment may have an investment in their own incapacity, because it can become the rationale for their own failure. The legitimation accorded them by non-disabled people is predicated on accepting responsibility for their incapacity, and not challenging the dominant order. Indeed, they may become token examples of the tragedy of disability, involved in consultations or wheeled out to highlight the problems.

(Shakespeare 1996: 100)

The point of this extended debate on identity is that it demonstrates the interconnections between cultural constructions, policy definitions and personal perceptions and the ways they reinforce each other. Disabled people need welfare because of the problems caused by their impairments, so common-sense wisdom tells us. It is obvious that the impairments cause us problems, otherwise we would not need welfare services. Small wonder, then, that disabled individuals internalise these ideas into the formation and maintenance of their identities.

Contesting constructions of disability

Despite the above, or maybe because of it, the notion of a positive disabled identity emerged from within the disabled people's movement itself, from disabled people coming together in their own organisations to discuss and evaluate their individual and collective experiences. Out of these discussions emerged a rejection of the negative implications of the individualistic medical approach to disability and a call for an emphasis on the exclusion and discrimination disabled people encounter daily. This shift in emphasis involves the replacing of one analytical framework – the 'medical model of disability' – with another: the 'social model of disability'.

The social model of disability is, first and foremost, a focus on the environmental and social barriers which exclude disabled people from mainstream society. It makes a clear distinction between impairment and disability. It is, therefore, a concerted attempt to direct attention to those aspects of disabled people's lives which can and should be changed. It is not a denial of the importance of impairment, appropriate medical intervention or, indeed, discussions of these experiences.

The disabled people's movement has, since its inception, always recognised and made provision for disabled people to talk about their experiences whether impairment- or disability-related. This re-evaluation of subjective experiences which follows an introduction to the social model often leads to a more positive perception of self. This is because the individual is no longer held primarily responsible for the economic and social deprivations they encounter daily. It involves the dual process of positive self-identification, and an affirmation of collective power.

But the process of transforming consciousness is not necessarily a cathartic one akin to religious conversion. It is often a slow and gradual process involving a re-evaluation of the individual's view of the world and their place within it. While this can be a private and individual development or personal awakening, it is more likely to take place in a collective context: collective self-organisation itself prompts the process of positive identification.

The gradual process of constructing positive disabled identities has meant that some elements in the media have started to reflect these changing constructions. For example, since the mid-1990s all of the major British soaps, including *Coronation Street*, *Brookside* and *East-Enders*, have included disabled characters. While many of these portrayals are decidedly lightweight – in the sense that they do not represent the everyday experiences of disabled people – there are a few where controversial disability issues have been addressed, but these are few and far between.

Moreover, for a brief period during 1994/5, news coverage focused on the denial of disabled peoples' rights rather than their perceived tragedies. But this can be explained with reference to two interrelated factors. First and foremost, the media's fascination for personal interest stories; in this case, the very public dispute between Sir Nicholas Scott, the then Minister for Disabled People, who was against the introduction of civil rights legislation, and his daughter, Victoria, who, as the secretary for the 'Rights Now' campaign, supported it. Second, the unprecedented growth of direct action and public demonstrations in support of anti-discrimination legislation by organisations of disabled people like the Disability Direct Action Network (DAN) (see below). Since then, however, although the campaign for effective civil rights legislation continues, media interest has waned, and the bulk of factual reporting has returned to less controversial and depressingly familiar themes.

While such positive identity-promoting activities have begun to have an impact on policy formation, and disabled people are gradually being seen as people requiring the right kind of support, much service provision remains locked into the idea of disabled people as in need of care. However, for many disabled people, rejecting care-based systems will not be possible until appropriate support-based systems become available to them. This is now beginning to happen and disabled people are in the forefront of building these support systems.

Constructing collective identities

The disabled people's movement has provided the collective framework for political identification. The re-evaluation of a disabled identity within a political context involves processes which challenge traditional views of disabled people as incapable, powerless and passive and, in so doing, establishes disabled people and their organisations as the 'experts' on disability and disability-related issues. As we have seen, this is in marked contrast to traditional policy and practice which has hitherto been dominated almost exclusively by personal tragedy theory and professional intervention. Indeed, it is the perceived failure of traditional approaches to disability that precipitated the emergence of the disabled people's movement in its present form.

Although the roots of this phenomenon can be traced back to the nineteenth century, with the setting up of the British Deaf Association (BDA) and the National League of the Blind (NLB) (Pagel 1988), it became a significant political force in the latter half of the 1960s. Key events include the struggle for greater autonomy by disabled residents in 'residential homes' for people with physical impairments (Hunt 1981; Finkelstein 1991) and the establishment in 1965 of the Disablement Incomes Group (DIG) by two disabled women to lobby against the poverty encountered by the majority of disabled people. But as the decade drew to a close, these initiatives were given a further boost by news of developments in Europe and America.

The emergence of the American Independent Living Movement (ILM) was especially important because it provided both an ideology and a practical solution to the problems faced by disabled people trying to live with inadequate and inappropriate welfare systems. Learning about the ILM and discovering that disabled people in other European states were struggling to achieve similar goals added to disabled people's growing knowledge and power, and began to reinforce their growing sense of collective social identity. This led to the emergence and proliferation throughout Britain during the 1970s of a variety of organisations controlled and run by disabled people. These included organisations which were overtly political from the start – the Union of Physically Impaired Against Segregation is probably the most notable example – and others which began life as self-help groups but which became involved in political activities through necessity rather than by design: for instance, the Spinal Injuries Association (SIA).

Initially a response to the British welfare system's failure to accommodate disabled people's needs, the primary aim of many of these organisations was to enable members 'to solve their problems themselves and not have them solved for them'. But the extent and the complexity of the problems faced, coupled with the opportunities these organisations gave for members to discuss and express their views, quickly led to the development of more political aims: to identify the needs of the membership as a whole and articulate them, both to statutory agencies, and to political parties at both a local and a national level. For example, besides providing services specifically for people with spinal cord injuries, the SIA has been at the centre of the campaign for equal rights for disabled people in Britain since the late 1970s. The SIA was formed in 1974 (Oliver and Hasler 1987).

However, in 1981 a handful of these organisations came together to form the British Council of Organisations of Disabled People (BCODP). Now known as the British Council of Disabled People, it has, since its inception, been at the forefront of the campaign for disabled people's rights both in Britain and in the international arena. For example, it was one of the founder members of the Disabled People's' International (DPI) in 1981; the DPI is its international equivalent with 113 member organisations from both rich and poor countries alike. As a consequence, the BCODP has become something of a catalyst for the politicisation of disabled people both in Britain and throughout Europe (Hurst 1995; Campbell and Olive 1996).

Its membership has increased substantially over the years; it currently stands at 123 organisations representing over 350 000 disabled individuals (BCODP 1997). Moreover:

> The move towards self-organisation has prompted increasing numbers of disabled people to adopt a shared political identity which in turn has helped to build a new mood of confidence. Disabled people no longer ask for change, but demand it. They are prepared to use a whole range of tactics in pursuit of their demands, including direct action and civil disobedience.
>
> (Oliver and Barnes 1991: 12)

The process of self re-evaluation occurring as part of a collective movement can take a variety of forms. Some individuals begin to reject dominant cultural values as children while others, following lengthy periods of denial, experience a cathartic realisation. The following two statements from disabled activists Micheline Mason and Rachel Hurst provide testimony to these contrasting experiences.

Like many disabled people, I have belonged to the disability movement since childhood. The day I threw away the Holy Water from Lourdes and said to

Jesus, 'I think they are missing the point', was the day I joined the movement. I was nine years old. I did not know if there were any other members then, or if it was just me and Him. Certainly there was no support from surrounding adults who told me I had very strange ideas. I lived in a world of my own, I was unrealistic, I must learn to face facts.

(cited in Campbell and Oliver 1996: 110)

In 1975 I experienced a conversion on 'the great road to Damascus' when I realised firstly that I was a disabled person, and secondly and almost instantaneously what discrimination was. I couldn't say that I could articulate it then as I can now but I knew that it was discrimination.

(cited in Campbell and Oliver 1996: 109)

One of the key mechanisms through which personal consciousness may be transformed is by sharing experiences with other people in similar situations or who face similar problems. As noted above, in the 1960s segregated institutions provided a fertile seedbed for disabled activists to foster a collective response to exclusion. Unlike other political movements such as the women's movement or the lesbian and gay movement who are united by a single characteristic such as gender or sexuality, disabled people are united only by their exclusion from mainstream society because of perceived impairments.

Hence, because different impairments have different effects, an emphasis on shared experiences often characterises initial encounters between disabled individuals during the process of politicisation. Elspeth Morrison explains:

In the early days, if you take the personal as political argument, then meetings were deeply political in that it was very much personal experiences which was getting people up and talking; about what it was like to have their particular impairment, what things disabled them, how the world saw them and what it felt to be like that.

(cited in Campbell and Oliver 1996: 108–9)

While an initial concern of the emerging disabled people's movement centred on social policy and welfare provision, the process of collective identity formation inevitably meant that a disability culture was also beginning to emerge. And, for many people, the process of self-re-evaluation begins by reading the work of other disabled writers. For instance, the following statement from a disabled woman, Fiona Campbell, illustrates the impact Jo Campling's (1981) edited collection of disabled women's writings had on her concept of disability:

As a woman with a disability [impairment], I see my own oppression and despair mirrored in the stories of all these women, but I also see, and I think any woman, and indeed any feminist, would see that, scattered here and there, and sometimes buried very deep, in the responses of these women to what society has done to them are some of the seeds of liberation.

(Campbell 1981: 8)

Of course the disabled people's movement has throughout its history recognised the need for appropriate forums for disabled people to share their experiences in order to facilitate the development of a positive reappraisal of self. One such forum was the journal *In from the Cold*. Edited and produced by five disabled members of the Liberation Network (see Document B in Part Two) and funded by donations, subscriptions and sales, this was the first 'liberation' magazine for disabled people in the UK. For more than six years this magazine provided a wealth of material including articles, reviews, news stories and cartoons, as well as detailed explorations of the experience of oppression by disabled individuals. At its height, the journal sold 1000 copies per issue and there is no doubt that it played a significant role in kick-starting disability culture.

Since the 1970s disabled activists have recognised the role of television as a means of transforming people's views about disability. In 1975 the independent television company ATV produced the Link programme. Although originally Link adopted a largely traditional approach to the subject, pioneering work by Rosalie Wilkins and Kevin Mulhearne, slowly but surely shifted the emphasis toward a more 'social model' approach. By 1987 almost all those working on the programme were disabled people. Indeed, as Vic Finkelstein has pointed out:

Link not only led the way for television programmes on disability issues but also provided a platform for some of us to develop our idea that disability is created by a world designed for able bodied living rather than by the way our bodies are impaired.

(Finkelstein 1996: 30)

Commensurate with the general shift toward programming for minorities, by the late 1980s other 'specialist' disability programmes had began to appear on British television including *Same Difference*, *See Hear*, and *One in Four*. In 1993 the British Broadcasting Corporation (BBC) set up the Disability Programmes Unit staffed in the main by disabled people, many of whom had learned the skills of media presentation with Link. Although it is difficult to quantify, there is anecdotal evidence that these developments have had some considerable impact on disabled people's consciousness as the following statement illustrates.

I've had my impairment from birth. It was only about six years ago that I came to accept my identity as a disabled person. I didn't particularly like disabled people. But one day I was watching the TV and it was these militant crips in the road in the USA. I thought, yeah, I can have some of that.

(Parker 1995: 6)

Becoming aware of the growing militancy among disabled people both in Britain and overseas has stimulated many individuals with impairments to adopt a 'disabled' identity, and become involved in direct political action. This can take a variety of forms. In the first half of the twentieth century disabled people were involved in conventional trade union activity. Blind people, organised by the National League of the Blind, were the most militant of all disabled groups during this period. They marched to London from all over Britain against poor working conditions in 1920, 1936 and 1948 (Humphries and Gordon 1992). In the early post-1948 period the formation of special interest groups such as the Disabled Drivers Association, formed in 1948, and the DIG are other examples of how disabled people began to engage directly in political activity. But the growth in self-organisation, combined with widespread frustration at the slowness of change, led to a more radical form of political participation in the 1980s and 1990s.

Much of the inspiration for this development comes from America: notably, the strategies adopted by the Civil Rights Movement and the ILM. The American Civil Rights movement of the 1960s had an enormous influence on the securing of disabled American's rights, and the manner by which those rights were secured. Indeed, when traditional legal channels were exhausted, 'disabled people . . . learned to employ other techniques of social protest. These included organised boycotts, sit ins and street demonstrations' (De Jong 1983: 12).

In Britain this type of action has increased dramatically over the last decade or so. Since the 'Rights not Charity' march of July 1988 there have been a growing number of demonstrations and civil disobedience campaigns by disabled people and their supporters up and down the country against a range of issues including inaccessible transport, an inaccessible environment, and the exploitation of disabled people by television companies and charities. The first major demonstration against Independent Television's charity show *Telethon* was in 1990. The next *Telethon*, two years later, drew over 2000 disabled demonstrators; it was the last. This and other successes precipitated the formation in 1993 of the Disability Direct Action Network (DAN). With a voluntary membership of over 1000 disabled individuals and no funding whatsoever apart from member's contributions, DAN has organised more than 100 local and national demonstrations.

This type of political activity has several important elements. First, it is a way of focusing attention on the institutions and environments that create disability; second, it is an overtly political act which demonstrates that disability is a matter of social relations, and not medical conditions; third, it is an opportunity for disabled individuals to get involved without the help of non-disabled people. But, above all, it is an empowering experience for disabled participants, creating a sense of solidarity, purpose and collective strength which enhances and develops a positive sense of self. As one participant at a DAN action in Cardiff in 1995 put it: 'The feeling of pride and power is unbelievable' (Parker 1996: 6).

Alongside political activism, cultural forms of self-expression, otherwise known as 'disability arts', emerged and became increasingly radical, helping to develop a sense of shared cultural identity which is central to the process of self re-evaluation. It is important to remember here that the link between perceived impairment and the arts is well-established within Western culture. Suffering, both physical and intellectual, for example, is widely regarded as an essential prerequisite for the creative process; many of the world's greatest artists, poets and musicians would today be regarded as disabled people.

What is crucial about the new disability arts movement, however, is that for the first time it is linked to a collective political movement producing both a culture of resistance and celebration at the same time. Such a culture has challenged much welfare provision which has often been tied to 'arts as therapy' in the processes of rehabilitation and care; painting, pottery, and basketry remain major activities in institutions for disabled people of all ages.

'Disability arts' represents a radical departure from these traditions in that it seeks to promote a cultural alternative to the dominance of personal tragedy theory within all aspects of Western culture. In short it: 'provides a context in which disabled people can get together, enjoy themselves and think in some way about issues of common concern. But it goes deeper than that, as disability culture really does offer people a key to the basic process of identifying as a disabled person, because culture and identity are closely linked concepts'.

(Vasey cited in Lees 1992: 13)

Since its emergence, disability arts and culture has contributed significantly to the growing mood of confidence among disabled people and, as a consequence, stimulated many to openly identify with the disabled people's movement. This is important because:

To encourage the growth of a disability culture is no less than to begin the radical task of transforming ourselves from passive and dependent beings into active and creative agents for social change.

(Morrison and Finkelstein, cited in Lees 1992: 22)

The emergence of this collective cultural identity has given countless disabled individuals the self-confidence to identify with the disabled people's movement, and to campaign for policies with which to bring about the development of a fairer and more just society. The circular constructions which have produced disabling culture, disabling welfare and internalised oppression have now been challenged and the implications of this not just for changing the face of welfare but also for transforming society are only now becoming apparent.

New social movements and the production of welfare

Elsewhere (Oliver 1990; Barnes 1991; Campbell and Oliver 1996) we have argued that the disabled people's movement can best be understood as one of the new social movements which are becoming increasingly important in late capitalist societies and that its significance, like that of other new social movements, is in its potential for transformation. At the individual level, this means transforming the personal into the political. At the social level, it means transforming a disabling culture and welfare system into a celebratory and liberating one. At the societal level, it means transforming society from an exclusionary into an inclusionary one.

Not all commentators who have studied new social movements in general would agree with our claims. It is sometimes suggested that movements like the disabled people's movement are not new at all but simply recent, contemporary examples of an age-old phenomena. It is also suggested that the significance of such movements is often over-stated and that in reality they are marginal components of the political system doomed ultimately to marginalisation or incorporation into the state. Finally it is sometimes argued that, in reality, the goals of these movements are much less ambitious than personal, social or political transformation.

Specifically in relation to social policy and disability, this position is taken by Fagan and Lee (1997) who state their general position as follows: 'All attempts to explain a series of quite divergent movements as a product of one set of, albeit complex, social changes must be questioned'(Fagan and Lee 1997: 145). Like Tom Shakespeare (1993) they suggest that the disabled people's movement's concern with civil rights means that it is really a movement for inclusive citizenship rather than one concerned with social transformation.

While not wishing to deny that inclusive citizenship is a key part of the strategy of the disabled people's movement, we have suggested here that the movement is much more than that and that full inclusive citizen-ship is not simply a matter of giving disabled people 'the same rights of citizenship as other groups enjoy' as Fagan and Lee (1996: 158) suggest.

Conclusion

In this chapter we have focused on the transformation of the concept of disability from the perspective of the disabled individual: in particular, the redefinition of self and a recognition that the personal is political. Central to this has been the rise of a collective social movement of disabled people which has sought to challenge existing cultural con-structions of disability, disabling welfare practices, and the internalised oppression of many disabled people, commensurate with these two factors. In the next and penultimate chapter we focus on the way in which these developments have begun to influence social policy for disabled people.

CHAPTER 7

Disability, policy and the way forward?

Introduction

Hitherto, we have focused on the ways in which the traditional, individualistic medical or 'personal tragedy' approach to social policy has shaped our understanding of disability as well as looking at the ways in which discourses and provision have been exclusionary. We have also focused on the burgeoning disabled people's movement and its impact on culture and the disabled population as a whole. Here we address the ways in which these developments have begun to influence social policy; in particular, the struggle for inclusion through the promotion of the idea of 'independent living'.

Our discussion centres on various initiatives which have emerged from within the disabled people's movement since the 1960s in order to facilitate this goal. These includes the call for a comprehensive disability income, the development of personal assistance schemes, and the on-going battle for effective civil rights legislation. We show that, taken together, these initiatives are indicative of the need for the further development of a bottom-up approach to community-based services, and a growing realisation among disabled people and their organisations that meaningful independent living can only be achieved through radical social change.

The campaign for a comprehensive disability income

When discussing alternatives to traditional personal tragedy approaches to social policy for disabled people in the post-1945 period it is appropriate to begin with the campaign for a comprehensive disability income. There are four reasons for this. First, the campaign was initiated by disabled people themselves rather than by professional policy-makers and experts. Second, when contextualised within the mid-twentieth century, the demand for a disability income represents a radical critique of conventional wisdom and policy in the disability field. Third, the colonisation of the campaign by non-disabled experts helped stimulate the growth of organisations controlled and run by disabled people. Fourth, the apparent limitations of the narrow incomes approach helped generate a more penetrating analysis focusing on the way society is organised.

The campaign for a comprehensive disability income gave rise to the formation in 1965 of the Disablement Incomes Group (DIG) by two disabled women: Berit Moore and Megan du Boisson. Initially, DIG was set up as a national association to 'consist of local groups dispersed throughout the country' whose activities were to be coordinated by a central organisation. Its purpose was:

> to work in general for the improvement of the social and economic condition of the disabled [*sic*], and, in particular, *for the provision by the state of a modest basic income, with special supplementary allowances, for all disabled persons ordinarily resident in the United Kingdom, whatever the cause of disablement, and irrespective of previous national insurance contributions.* (original emphasis)
> (DIG 1965: 1)

The significance of this grass-roots initiative can only be properly understood when located in the Britain of the mid-1960s. This was a period of relative economic stability and growing affluence, political consensus in terms of the further development of state welfare, and a general feeling of optimism for the future among the population as a whole. The United Kingdom had finally recovered from the lingering postwar austerity of the late 1940s and 1950s, and the British people had been told and, in the main, believed that they 'had never had it so good'.

In contrast, the situation for disabled people was not so rosy; as we have seen 'community care' policies were in their infancy and disability benefits were non-existent. While some community-based services had existed during the first half of the twentieth century these were mainly *ad hoc* and characterised by wide parochial variations. In short, disabled people were not being included in the rising living standards that were now being experienced by most other sectors of society. In terms of benefits, until the 1970s state-funded welfare payments were focused mainly on people with acquired conditions caused by war or industrial accident, and who had a qualifying record of National Insurance contributions. Until this time disabled people not eligible for any form of compensatory benefits had to rely entirely on means-tested National Assistance payments.

The idea of a national comprehensive disability income quickly emerged and was promoted as the way to ensure that disabled people were able to share in the affluence of the period and as the way to ensure their inclusion into society. To put it crudely: if poverty was the problem disabled people faced, giving them money was perceived as the solution. Clearly, a radical initiative at the time, the DIG was responsible for a great deal of policy development on the disability income field and they organised a major rally in Trafalgar Square in 1968 in support of their campaign for a national disability income (Campbell and Oliver 1996: 152).

However, the campaign also attracted the attention of a plethora of non-disabled experts and organisations controlled and run by non-disabled people. The DIG's concentration on the incomes issue inevitably led to a focus on Parliamentary lobbying by a small group of mainly non-disabled experts while the majority of its members remained largely passive. Although some limited success was achieved, notably the introduction of the Attendance Allowance, a fully comprehensive national disability income seemed light years away. To give more muscle to the campaign the Disability Alliance (DA) – an umbrella body for disability organisations both of and for disabled people – was formed in 1974. Primarily concerned with 'public education' and the production and distribution of information about the poverty associated with disability, the DA according to Peter Townsend, one of its founders, was a 'more authoritative body . . . in the sense that it could decently claim to be speaking on behalf of the majority of organisations concerned with disabled people' (UPIAS 1976: 5).

As well as being anti-democratic in the sense that the organisations concerned with the incomes approach were not properly representative ones, the campaign was also somewhat naïve in its assumption that providing evidence of the poverty of disabled people would be enough to stir governments into action. Finally, the campaign failed to recognise that a national disability income might itself be exclusionary; if disabled people were to be provided with an adequate income without working, there would be no need to include disabled people in the labour market and in the workforce.

The failure to address such basic issues stimulated criticism of both the DIG and the DA from the more 'populist' organisations of disabled people, notably the Union of Physically Impaired Against Segregation (UPIAS) which had been formed in 1972. The Union was set up by disillusioned disabled activists following a letter written by Paul Hunt and published in the *Guardian* newspaper on 20 September 1972. It functioned mainly through confidential correspondence and circulars circulated among its members. This literature had to be confidential because many UPIAS members were living in institutions and 'it was important that they could share their thoughts and experiences, and speak freely without fear of retribution' (Campbell and Oliver 1996: 66).

The views expressed in UPIAS literature resulted in the formulation of the UPIAS Policy Statement and constitution first adopted in 1974 and later amended in 1976 (see Document A in Part Two). In contrast to the narrow incomes approach of the DIG and the DA, Union members were adamant that first, disability should be considered as a totality and that no single aspect could be treated in isolation; and second, that disabled people must be able to control their own lives with the support they needed. For the UPIAS, it was evident that the incomes approach concentrated on the symptom – the poverty of disabled people, and not the cause, the disabling society in which we live – and that both the DIG and DA had moved away from representing disabled people, but instead presented an 'expert view of the problem'. The logical outcome of such an approach would simply make matters worse rather than better (UPIAS 1976).

Furthermore, it was argued that a 'narrow incomes approach' would inevitably necessitate some kind of assessment process which would legitimate and perpetuate the discriminatory practices of the past. Disabled individuals wishing to claim the disability income would be required to present themselves for assessment by 'social administrators'. They would have to appear 'passive, nervous' and 'deferential' in order to conform to the expert view of disability; in other words, they would have to reinforce all the traditional assumptions associated with disabled people, and thus relinquish any claim to economic and social equality. Such an approach can only enhance the power of professionals and justify the continued subordination of disabled people. A few of the more privileged disabled individuals might be cast into the role of token 'expert'. But the whole strategy would perpetuate the historical and traditional situation whereby disabled people are made dependent on the thinking and decisions of others (UPIAS 1976: 18).

In contrast, the Union called for the introduction of a wide range of radical policies. These included the necessary state funding and support to enable disabled people to gain maximum independence in daily living activities, achieve nobility, undertake productive work and to live where and how they choose with full control over their lives.

Beyond the incomes approach

As a consequence of the activities of the DIG and the UPIAS a number of initiatives emerged during the 1970s and 1980s which posed a direct challenge to the exclusionary policies of the past. One of the first was the Disablement Information and Advice Line (DIAL) initiated by disabled activists in Derbyshire. The setting up of DIAL is significant because it was evident to disabled activists that disabled people did not have access to the information necessary to facilitate their empowerment; in other words, information is power. Because people with impairments have been excluded from the mainstream of community life they needed specialist information in addition to that needed by everyone else.

Despite repeated government recognition of such a need, both the National Assistance Act 1948 and the Chronically Sick and Disabled Persons Act 1970 instructed local authorities to provide appropriate information to disabled people, notably, about community-based services. It was apparent that such services were not widely available. The situation was particularly acute for people living in rural areas.

This led to the setting up of the first Disablement Information and Advice Line in Derbyshire in 1976. This was a telephone and advice service initiated by disabled residents living in Cressy Fields, a Derbyshire residential home and day centre, with a small grant from Derbyshire County Council. The service, run by disabled volunteers from a converted cloakroom, was a milestone in the development of the local disabled people's movement (Davis and Mullender 1993).

Moreover, DIAL Derbyshire quickly caught the imagination of others. Similar services were set up in Manchester, London and other parts of the country. By 1978 a steering committee had been formed from representatives of local DIAL groups to form a National Association of Disablement Information and Advice Services, now known colloquially as DIAL UK. Its aim was to facilitate the spread of a network of local services so that disabled people are not disabled because of lack of intelligible information and informed advice anywhere in the UK.

The spread of such organisations made a significant contribution to the empowerment of the disabled population. For example, by 1980 DIAL Derbyshire had handled some 5000 queries and was intimately aware of local concerns, local issues and the aspirations of local disabled people. The disabled activists involved were able to speak with authority about local problems. Most importantly, they were also able to develop clear ideas about solutions:

DIAL Derbyshire had become a base, a focal point of disability activity, and it took the gradual process of disabled people 'coming together', which had been developing for over twenty years, an important stage further. Its link with the local authority also helped to pave the way for more comprehensive developments which were to come.

(Davis and Mullender 1993: 8)

It is important to note, however, that soon after its inception DIAL UK was quickly colonised by non-disabled professionals and is no longer an organisation controlled and run by disabled people. Moreover, the lion's share of funding for information services goes to national disability information providers, the majority of which are controlled and run by non-disabled people. Furthermore, most local user-led organisations providing this type of service survive with only the most meagre of resources. Consequently, provision remains limited and varies considerably in different parts of the country (Barnes 1995).

However, another early initiative from within the Derbyshire area was the Grove Road Scheme. This was an integrated housing complex conceived and developed by disabled people while they were still living in institutions. Beginning in 1972, the initiative took four years to develop. It involved detailed and sometimes difficult negotiations with Housing Associations, the District Council, the Local Authority Social Services Department, and architects and planners. On completion, the Grove Road complex resembled little more than a group of six ordinary looking flats. But inside, the three ground-floor properties featured designs and adaptations now commonly associated with 'wheelchair' or 'accessible housing': housing which is designed for, or easily convertible for, use by wheelchair users. The three first-floor flats were designed to be let to non-disabled families willing to cooperate with the disabled tenants in order to provide appropriate support when needed.

Clearly, a reaction to the experience of exclusion inside an institution, the principal objective behind the Grove Road scheme was that it should not be conspicuous, but must blend into the local community and cater for disabled people's needs in the privacy of their own homes in a way which encourages and supports independence and individuality. Not only did the Grove Road project provide a suitable housing environment for both disabled and non-disabled people, it also provided empirical evidence that given the right support, people with 'severe' physical impairments were perfectly able to live independently in a community-based setting; to be fully included into society, given the right kind and level of support.

Independent living, centres for independent/integrated living, and personal assistance schemes

Around this time news of the American Independent Living Movement (ILM) began to filter through to disabled people in Britain. This was particularly important because developments in the USA provided evidence of what disabled people in the UK knew already; that the obstacles to their self-fulfilment were the direct outcome of living in hostile physical and social environments and that current services were inhibiting rather than empowering.

The American ILM had emerged in the early 1970s, partly from within the campus culture of American universities and partly from repeated efforts by American disability organisations to influence US disability legislation (Anspach 1979; De Jong 1983; Hahn 1986). During the 1960s various 'self-help' programmes had been introduced by some American universities to enable students with 'severe' physical impairments to attend mainstream courses. But it was not until the early 1970s that the movement gained validity and momentum with the creation of the first Centre for Independent Living (CIL) in Berkeley, California.

The Berkeley CIL incorporated itself in 1972 as a self-help group to be managed by disabled people. It provided a wide range of related services including 'peer counselling, advocacy services, transportation, training in independent living skills, attendance care referral, wheelchair repair, and others'. It had no residential facilities and catered for people with a wide variety of impairments, many of whom were extremely severe (De Jong 1983).

As CILs developed they responded to the needs of the local community, and as a consequence, sometimes provided a different range of services. In 1993 there were over 200 CILs operating in the USA (Evans 1993). Further, there are now CILs in most 'developed' countries such as Australia, Canada, Japan, various European states including Britain, and also in several 'developing' nations of the majority world such as Brazil and Zimbabwe (Ratzka 1992: 23–5).

However, the situation in America, where CILs emerged, is distinct from that in the UK in at least three important respects. First, America has long had a tradition of viewing some social problems as human rights issues, both in terms of constitutional history and the influence of the civil rights movement. Second, there were very few statutory services available to disabled people. Third, there was no large organised voluntary sector 'for the disabled'.

By contrast, in Britain there was no human rights tradition and there was and still remains a veritable farrago of state-run services for disabled people, and a large well-established voluntary sector, elements of which date back to the nineteenth century. In several respects, therefore, the problem for the British disabled people's movement was less to do with creating services and more to do with controlling them. For some, this warranted a change of name from Centres for Independent Living to Centres for Integrated Living and a change in tactics.

Indeed, Britain's first CILs were set up in the early 1980s by two pioneering disabled people's organisations: the Derbyshire Coalition of Disabled People (DCDP), and the Hampshire Coalition of Disabled People (HCDP). The DCDP was formally established in 1981 by disabled activists from DIAL Derbyshire following on from the International Year of Disabled People (IYDP). From the outset the idea of setting up a CIL in Derbyshire was given the highest priority. But it was not until 1985 that the Derbyshire Centre for Integrated Living (DCIL) was registered as an independent autonomous company.

The delay was due to several factors: notably, protracted discussions within the Coalition, with other disabled people's organisations, both inside and outside the UK, and with the local Council on what form the new CIL should take. Since its inception DCIL has gone 'from strength to strength' (Oliver 1987) and despite severe funding cutbacks in the early 1990s, continues to provide a wide range of services commensurate with the needs of local disabled people.

An alternative approach was adopted by disabled people in Hampshire. 'Project 81: Consumer Directed Housing and Care' grew out of *ad hoc* discussions among disabled people living in a residential home, Le Court, run by the Leonard Cheshire Foundation in 1979. Drawing extensively on the experience of disabled people in other parts of the country and overseas – notably, the American ILM – the Project 81 management committee persuaded the local authority that the resources used to finance 'residential care' for disabled people could just as easily be used to support them in the community. This would include sufficient funding to adapt houses for use by disabled individuals and to enable them to employ their own personal assistant, helper or 'carer' to do the things they were unable to do for themselves.

In contrast to established, professionally dominated practices, the Project 81 group maintained that the disabled person should be responsible for assessing their own support needs. These needs might include 'personal care needs' – getting up, washing, using the toilet, and so on; 'domestic matters' – cleaning the house, laundry, shopping, cooking, etc. and 'social care' – support for employment, leisure activities and so on. This was something that disabled people living in institutions could not and still never can hope to achieve.

The Project 81 group were also responsible for setting up the Hampshire Centre for Independent Living (HCIL) in 1985, the same year that the DCIL came into existence. From the outset HCIL endeavoured to provide a community-based resource, not only for disabled people hoping to leave institutions, but also for those already living in the community struggling to survive and under the threat of going into 'residential care'. While HCIL's primary focus revolved around personal assistance use, information, advocacy and training in 'independent living skills' were also provided. This gave disabled people the resources and confidence 'to survive in the community' (Evans 1993: 23).

Over the years HCIL have published several personal assistance user manuals and papers (see for example HCIL, *Papers* 1990). They were also responsible for the setting up and distribution of a free newsletter for personal assistance users: *The Personal Assistance Newsletter*, a responsibility which was taken on by the British Council of Disabled People (BCODP) in 1991. At the time of writing (November 1997) there are more than 530 personal assistance users in Hampshire (Mason 1997). And, despite considerable resistance from professionals and their organisations, there are 12 CILs operating in different parts of the country providing a range of services commensurate with the needs of local disabled people (BCODP 1997).

Financing independent living

Under Section 29 of the National Assistance Act 1948 it was illegal for local authorities to provide funding directly to disabled individuals to employ their own personal assistants. The Project 81 group overcame this problem by suggesting that funding could be made available to a suitable organisation or third party, in this case the Le Court Residential Home, who would then administer it to the disabled individual. After lengthy negotiations the authority agreed to the proposal and one by one the residents moved out of the institution and into the community (Evans 1993) – the first left Le Court in 1982.

This pioneering development gave rise to other initiatives by disabled people and their organisations and, since the early 1980s, there has been a steady increase in the availability of payment schemes throughout the UK. Some of these were similar to the original Hampshire model in that payments were administered by a 'third party' such as a local voluntary organisation or a trust set up specifically for this purpose. Some local authorities even elected to make cash payments direct to the disabled individual. But this practice declined significantly in the early 1990s, following government reminders that such payments were in fact illegal (Zarb and Nadash 1994).

However, the influence of initiatives by disabled people and their organisations is clearly evident in government policy-making during the 1980s. For instance, user involvement in the planning and delivery of local services was enshrined in law with the Disabled Persons (Services, Consultation and Representation) Act 1986, although it is important to remember that this particular piece of legislation was never fully implemented. But the most significant example was the setting up of the Independent Living Fund (ILF) in 1988.

The ILF came into existence due mainly to pressure from disabled people's organisations over the inflexibility of the new benefit system following the implementation of the Social Security Act 1986. Originally intended as a purely temporary measure, the ILF represented the first large-scale opportunity for disabled people to access money to satisfy their individual support needs, rather than rely on those provided by their family and friends, local authorities or voluntary agencies.

The ILF covered the whole country and had no connection with local services. While payments were originally intended to cover only domestic support, the criteria were quickly changed to enable people to purchase personal assistance. Most importantly, unlike local authorities who were only able to make indirect payments, funding from the ILF went directly to the disabled individual (Kestenbaum 1993; Zarb and Nadash 1994).

Applicants to the ILF were means tested and assessments of need were determined by non-disabled social worker 'experts'. Assessments were geared toward personal and domestic needs only; social needs, say for support at work, for example, were not taken into account. Moreover, payments did not cover management or administration costs: examples include, advertising, training, insurance costs, and the wage levels used in the assessment process were based on the lowest possible estimates. Hence, ILF recipients were forced into paying subsistence wages and were also prohibited from employing family or friends as personal assistants (Barnes 1991).

Inevitably, and despite serious misgivings within the disabled people's movement about how the ILF was administered and operated, it proved to be incredibly popular with disabled people. Despite the difficulties mentioned above, the inescapable fact remained that giving disabled people cash gave them far more autonomy and freedom in their lives than professionally controlled services ever had.

Although it was originally estimated that there would only be around 300 new awards a year, with a maximum of 1250 overall, these forecasts were soon overtaken by demand. After only one year, applications exceeded 900 a month and by November 1992 this had risen to 2000 a month. By the time the original fund ceased operations in spring 1993, there were a total of 22 000 disabled people receiving payments; evidence also suggests that this figure would have risen further had the fund continued to operate (Lakey 1994; Zarb and Nadash 1994).

In 1992 the government announced that the ILF would be closed from the end of March 1993 to coincide with the implementation of the 1990 community care reforms. It was replaced by two new charitable trusts: the Independent Living (Extension) Fund, which continues to make payments to existing users, and the Independent Living (1993) Fund. The latter was set up to run alongside the services provided or purchased by local authorities.

It differed from the original ILF in several crucial ways. First, it was administered locally: whereas applications used to be made direct to the ILF, now they were to be dealt with by local authorities' Social Services

Departments. Second, payments were to be linked to the use of local services; applicants must be in receipt of services worth more than £200 per week before they could apply. Payments of up to £300 could then be used to purchase additional support to supplement services. Hence, the total cost of support was cash limited to a ceiling of £500. This meant that people whose support package exceeded the £500 limit lived under the constant threat of being forced to go into residential care.

The limitations of the new ILF intensified the call from disabled people's organisations and their supporters that local authorities should be empowered to make direct payments for personal assistance to disabled individuals. Indeed, extensive research on the experience of direct payments, pioneered by both disabled researchers and disabled people's organisations, shows that enabling disabled people to organise their own support system offers much more control, flexibility and choice than direct service provision.

These studies also highlight the ways in which this higher level of control creates greater opportunities for disabled individuals to enter the labour market, participate in mainstream social and leisure activities, and reduces their dependence on family and friends. They also demonstrate that, in many cases, payment schemes represent considerable cost savings compared to both community-based services and residential care (Oliver and Zarb 1992; Morris 1993; Philips 1993; Lakey 1994; Zarb and Nadash 1994).

The strength of these arguments, coupled with intensive lobbying by disabled people and their organisations – notably, the BCODP's Independent Living Committee – prompted the campaign for a change in the law to allow local authorities to make direct payments for personal assistance to disabled individuals. The Community Care (Direct Payments) Act 1996 became law on 1 April 1997.

Although not mandatory it allows local authorities to make payments directly to disabled individuals eligible for community care services who wish to organise their own support system and employ personal assistants. In November 1997 there were at least 76 known personal assistance schemes, many of which are run by disabled people, operating up and down the UK (NCIL 1997). The 1996 Act is by no means perfect – local authorities are not obliged to make direct payments and, as yet, people over 65 are not eligible for these schemes (see Document N in Part Two) – but it does represent a major step forward in disabled people's on-going struggle for inclusion into the mainstream of British society.

Civil rights for disabled people

Another important element in the quest for inclusion is the continuing battle for effective civil rights legislation for disabled people. It will be clear from the above that independent living is about far more than disabled people having control over disability services and personal assistance schemes. It is about 'access, access to schools, jobs, transport, houses, public buildings, leisure etc. – all the things that non-disabled people take for granted' (Bracking 1993: 14). It is often argued that the introduction of comprehensive civil rights legislation would go some way to achieve these goals.

In the British context, one of the first people to address the issue of discrimination against disabled people was the disabled activist Paul Hunt. In *A Critical Condition* (1966) Hunt drew parallels between the experience of disabled people and other 'minority groups' such as Black people, lesbians, and gay men, and suggested that, like them, disabled people encounter 'discrimination and oppression' (p. 152). But the type of discrimination encountered by disabled people is not simply a question of direct discrimination or prejudice: it is, as we have seen in previous chapters, 'institutionalised in the very fabric of British society' (Barnes 1991) and finds expression in the systematic exclusion of disabled people from mainstream economic and social activities.

From the mid-1970s onwards, organisations controlled and run by disabled people such as UPIAS, the Liberation Network, and the early disabled women's movement in the form of Sisters Against Disability (SAD), all shared the same basic goals: namely, to secure equal rights for disabled people, and to remove negative discrimination in all its forms. Similar goals were later adopted by the BCODP following its inception in 1981. As noted in Chapter 6, a member of Disabled People's International (DPI), from the outset, the BCODP is Britain's national umbrella for organisations of disabled people. Initiated by members of the UPIAS, it had representatives from only seven national organisations at its first meeting. With remarkably few resources its influence has been considerable in the struggle for disabled people's rights.

However, the first steps to getting some form of anti-discrimination legislation (ADL) on to the Parliamentary agenda were taken not by the UPIAS or the BCODP but by the Committee on Restrictions Against Disabled People (CORAD). The Committee was established by the then Labour government in 1979 following the findings of the Report of the Silver Jubilee Access Committee (SJAC). The CORAD Report located the problem of discrimination within a structural or institutional context. The committee examined a wide range of issues such as access to public buildings, transport systems, education, employment and entertainment. They also made a number of important recommendations for improving public attitudes toward disabled people and called for the introduction of ADL to secure disabled people's rights by law.

When CORAD began its work in 1979, there was a degree of optimism among disabled people that its recommendations would find their way on to the statute books. After all, CORAD was a government-sponsored committee and the United Nations had designated 1981 the International Year of Disabled People. But the political climate changed considerably following the election in May 1979 of the Conservative government under the premiership of Margaret Thatcher. Hence, by the time the CORAD Report was published in 1982, the chances of any meaningful anti-discrimination bill becoming law had greatly diminished (Davis 1996). Nonetheless, the first unsuccessful attempt was made on 6 July 1982 by the deaf MP, Jack Ashley. Thirteen years and 14 attempts later the now-discredited 1995 Disability Discrimination Act (DDA) entered the British statute books.

Enhanced pressure to bring about a change in the law came from a variety of sources both outside and inside the UK. For instance, government responsibility for securing equal rights for disabled people was stated in the UN *World Programme of Action Concerning Disabled Persons* which was adopted by consensus in the UN General Assembly in 1982. It explicitly recognises the right of all human beings to equal opportunities and is a major extension of the concept of human rights (UN 1988).

Another important influence was the passing into law of the Americans With Disabilities Act (ADA) on 26 July 1990, following a long and vigorous campaign by disabled Americans. Arguably the most comprehensive anti-discrimination policy yet introduced anywhere in the world, subsequently several other countries including Australia, China, France, New Zealand have put some form of civil rights legislations for disabled people on to the statute books. All this has added considerable weight to disabled people's continuing struggle for equal treatment within the UK.

In Britain the campaign for civil rights for disabled people grew in stature during the 1980s with the formation in 1985 of the Voluntary Organisations for Anti-Discrimination Legislation (VOADL) committee. This signified a coming together of organisations of disabled people, such as the BCODP, along with the more traditional organisations for disabled people like the Royal Association for Disability and Rehabilitation (RADAR). VOADL was important because it signified the public conversion of several of the larger organisations for disabled people to the idea of civil rights legislation.

The production of the BCODP report on discrimination (Barnes 1991) subsequently provided the most extensive quantitative and qualitative evidence on the extent of discrimination against disabled people yet produced in the UK. Further, before the book's publication the British government were still denying that discrimination against the disabled was a major problem. Five days after its official launch in a House of Commons debate on the tenth attempt to get ADL through Parliament, the government's then Minister for Disabled People, Nicholas Scott, admitted for the first time that 'discrimination against disabled people is widespread' (Hansard 1992).

Besides the unprecedented growth of organisations controlled and run by disabled people, other important contributory factors include the development of 'disability arts' and the emergence of disability culture as a potent political force; the generation and widespread use by disabled people of a radical new method of consciousness-raising based on the social model of disability known as Disability Equality Training

(DET) (Gillespie-Sells and Campbell 1991): and the politicisation and subsequent radicalisation of increasingly large sections of the disabled population (see Chapter 6). These and innumerable other initiatives intensified the pressure for nothing less than the full inclusion of disabled people with comprehensive civil rights legislation as the main vehicle for its achievement.

By the mid-1990s the pressure had intensified substantially and it was clear that the campaign for civil rights was unstoppable. Given their entrenched position it was inevitable, however, that the government would 'try to hold its established policy line with a pre-emptive legislative strike designed to avoid more radical measures' (Davis 1994: 247). This came at the end of 1994 with the introduction of the Conservative government's Disability Discrimination Bill. Organisations of disabled people, led by the BCODP, branded the Bill as weak and toothless, and reaffirmed their commitment to a more comprehensive and enforceable civil rights policy. But the Bill received Royal Ascent on 8 December 1995.

The Disability Discrimination Act (DDA) 1995 is weak because it is based on the traditional individualistic medical view of disability: impairment is the cause of disablement rather than the way society is organised. Hence, the idea that disabled people's legitimate requests for adjustments and change are considered somehow unrealistic and unnecessary is retained. The Act gives only limited protection from direct discrimination in employment, the provision of goods and services, and in the selling or letting of land. Protection is limited because not all disabled people are covered by the Act, and employers and service providers are exempt if they can show that compliance would damage their business.

Most importantly, the Act is toothless because there is no enforcement mechanism whatsoever. This means that disabled individuals must challenge unfair discrimination themselves. Instead, there is a National Disability Council (NDC); its role is to 'advise' the government on implementation but not with reference to employment. This responsibility falls to the existing National Advisory Council on Employment of People with Disabilities (NACEPD). The chair of the NDC works on disability issues one day a week; the other 16 members one day a month.

Significantly, the coming of the DDA put an end to the uneasy alliance between organisations of and organisations for disabled people which began with the establishment of the VOADL Committee and continued when it changed its name to Rights Now in 1992. Shortly after the inception of the NDC, six of the main organisations for disabled people – RADAR, the National Institute for the Blind, the National Institute for the Deaf, MENCAP, MIND and SCOPE – agreed to work with the government to implement the new law. Despite protestations to the contrary by prominent representatives of these organisations, this action only served to undermine the on-going struggle for the introduction of a meaningful and effective civil rights policy.

Inevitably, such a policy must emphasise social rights rather than individual needs and, therefore, focus on the disabling society in which we live and not on individual disabled people. It must ensure disabled people's right to life and appropriate health care. This means the regulation and control of the eugenic impulse which governs genetic medicine, and an end to selective abortion on the basis of impairment and the withholding of life saving medical treatments to people with 'severe' impairments. It must also secure disabled people's right to sexual relationships, marriage and parenthood. It must give disabled people the right and resources to challenge discrimination in all its forms in mainstream education, employment, the built environment – housing, public amenities and transport – and in the provision of goods and services. It must also ensure that disabled people are empowered to reject enforced institutionalisation and that they have access to the support needed to live independently within the community.

Moreover, for such a policy to be truly effective it must be accompanied by first, a meaningful freedom of information act to ensure that medical records and other information can no longer be used to legitimate prejudice and ignorance; and second, a strong and independent enforcement mechanism which offers disabled people individual and collective redress. It is crucial that any enforcement mechanism be independent of government influence and control; experience shows that the effectiveness of government-sponsored commissions and councils is easily manipulated by Parliamentary control of funding and appointments: the experience of the Commissions for Racial Equality, Equal Opportunities, and the National Disability Council illustrate the point well. This can only be accomplished, therefore, by the adequate funding of the nationwide network of organisations controlled and run by disabled people themselves. It is these organisations which have put the issue of disabled people's rights on to the political agenda and it is these organisations which are best placed to secure those rights.

But, as we have argued elsewhere (Oliver 1990; Barnes 1991), it is important to remember that, by themselves, none of these policies will prove successful. First, ADL without freedom of information and a supportive network of disabled people will simply benefit the legal profession. Second, access to information by itself will almost certainly expose disabled individuals to further professional mystification and exploitation. Third, support for organisations of disabled people without an appropriate framework which guarantees basic human rights will effectively neutralise the only collective voice that disabled people have in the UK. But an integrated policy similar to that suggested here would provide an appropriate means by which the systematic exclusion of disabled people can be addressed effectively and, as a consequence, make a significant contribution to its eventual eradication.

Conclusion

In this chapter we have focused on disabled people's struggle for inclusion into the mainstream of British society. From the mid-twentieth century onwards this has, in a variety of ways, warranted a gradual but increasingly radical reappraisal of policy-making in the general area of disability. From relatively small beginnings and with remarkably limited resources, disabled people and their organisations have successfully challenged professional wisdom and intransigence. In so doing, they have generated a range of policy initiatives enabling ever-increasing numbers of disabled people to live independently within the local community. But this independence remains limited by a variety of environmental and social barriers and, consequently, the struggle for inclusion must continue.

The evidence also suggests that a successful outcome might only be achieved by the further development of a bottom-up approach to policy-making, and a general acceptance that meaningful inclusion for disabled people and, indeed, for other disadvantaged groups, is only possible through deep-rooted and radical changes in the way our society is organised.

CHAPTER 8

Welfare state, welfare society?

Introduction

In this book we have addressed the ways in which established approaches to state-sponsored welfare, with particular emphasis on the British experience, has effectively included and excluded disabled people from the mainstream of community life as well as discussing our collective response to this exclusion. Here we draw together the various strands of our argument and maintain that, despite the ambiguities and contradictions thrown up by the welfare state, it remains an essential ingredient for the development of a truly inclusionary society. This is a global society in which both disabled and non-disabled people can participate and realise their full potential and where the notion of disability and all its associate deprivations are little more than a dim and distant memory.

For us, a vision of how things should and ought to be is fundamental to all social analysis. This was certainly the driving force underpinning the bulk of the work produced by the key figures associated with the development of the social sciences during the nineteenth and first half of the twentieth centuries. Sadly, it is a feature conspicuous by its absence from so much of what constitutes social theorising over the last few years with its quest for the complexities of the meaning of life without much concern with how to change these meanings. Our own view is not dissimilar to that of Marx who chastised the German idealist philosophers for merely interpreting the world instead of trying to change it.

It is very likely that those responsible for this trend will argue that there are numerous and complex explanations for such omissions. But two significant factors are undoubtedly the rise of the 'new right' in both Britain and America during the early 1980s and the subsequent 'triumph' of capitalism over communism following the collapse of Eastern bloc countries at the end of that particular decade. Since then, with one or two notable exceptions (George and Wilding 1994; Leonard 1997), political and academic expediency has prompted many social theorists of social policy to abandon almost completely discussions of and the search for social justice and the 'good society' with a modern welfare state as its centrepiece.

The future of the welfare state

According to John Hills (1995) in his study of the future of welfare for the Joseph Rowntree Foundation, there are three options open to us.

First, we can maintain or even improve provision in relation to both need and contemporary living standards, by accepting a slow rise in the share of welfare spending in gross domestic product (GDP) and, hence, in the taxes to pay for it. Second, we can keep welfare spending down by continuing to link benefits to prices and not incomes, although this may not be politically achievable or acceptable as the poor get poorer. Third, we can maintain the value of certain items but cut out or reduce support for others; this will mean that priorities will need to be identified and hard choices made.

Not all the political parties find this incremental and reformist approach acceptable. Building on new right critiques of the welfare state, David Green suggests that 'By narrowing opportunities for personal idealism in the service of others, the welfare state has eroded the sense of personal responsibility and mutual obligation on which a resilient civil society rests' (Green 1993: viii). While we would accept that a major problem with state welfare is that it has created dependency rather than allowed for the expression of collective altruism among the population as a whole, mutual obligation under Green's scenario is a euphemism for charity and, therefore, unacceptable to the organised voice of disabled people: the disabled people's movement.

The 'new left' also suggest that minor reform of the existing welfare state is not enough. Tony Giddens, for example, provides nothing less than a critique of modernity itself and suggests that the welfare state has failed to adapt to the changing conditions of what he calls the 'post-scarcity society'. This can be done by integrating a wider set of life concerns than those of productivism and thereby developing a politics of second chances. A range of social pacts or settlements can also be created in the new stakeholder society and all this can be done through 'generative politics as the main means of effectively approaching problems of poverty and social exclusion in the present day' (Giddens 1994: 15). The problem with this for disabled people, and for other socially excluded groups, as we go on to argue, is that the party political system has hitherto shown itself incapable of representing such a wide disparity of needs and aspirations. This, for us, is important because if social analysis is unable to provide any kind of insight into what such a society should and ought to look like, and the policies with which to achieve it, there is little point in doing it. As Oscar Wilde so cogently pointed out over a century ago in *The Soul of Man Under Socialism* (first published in 1890): 'a map of the world that does not include Utopia (what we have termed the Good Society) is not even worth glancing at . . . Progress is the realisation of Utopias' (Wilde 1966: 1090).

In our view, neither of these approaches sees the need to transform rather than reform capitalism and, accordingly, provide only limited visions of what the welfare state might look like under re-energised capitalism (Green) or reformed modernity (Giddens).

However, we return to what we consider constitutes the good society at the end of this chapter. For the moment it is sufficient to point out that a glimpse of the good society, and an outline of the kind of policies needed to accomplish it, can be found in the writings of disabled people and their organisations. What we now need to consider are the possibilities for change under the middle way or centrist approach of Britain's New Labour government.

The limits of possibility or limitless possibilities

One of the first things Margaret Thatcher said, as head of a 'new right' government when she came to power in 1979, was that disabled people could not expect to be exempt from any necessary changes that were going to be made in the welfare state. Students of recent political history will be struck by the remarkable similarity with a statement made by Tony Blair in his introduction to planned reforms in the welfare state by his New Labour government when they took office on May 1 1997. For us, both of these attempts lack a vision of the possible: merely tinkering with some bits of the welfare state, notably benefits, is likely to reinforce exclusion rather than facilitate inclusion.

The Thatcherite attempt, based on the twin strategies of marketisation and public expenditure reduction, failed because markets proved no more efficient in allocating resources than professional definitions of need and because benefits, once given, are very hard to take away. It would be a mistake, however, to imagine that history was about to repeat itself and for two very important reasons. First, while Tony Blair is in a stronger position than Margaret Thatcher was, unlike the Tories who were either ambivalent to or profoundly against the welfare state, New Labour is broadly supportive of it. Second, when the Tories came to power, there was no powerful and committed disabled people's movement to defend the interests of disabled people.

The New Labour government, just like the previous Tory one, in rightly seeking to reform the welfare state, wrongly sees reform as synonymous with cuts in expenditure. As we go on to argue, cutting cash benefits is likely to lock disabled people further into dependency on the state and, therefore, be exclusionary rather inclusionary: what is needed to empower them to become fully participating citizens is a new, vibrant democracy with as its centrepiece, a modern welfare state.

A central plank in New Labour's strategy, which does differ markedly from the plans of their predecessors, is its welfare to work programme: a strategy based on a similar policy introduced by President Bill Clinton in the USA. This could certainly have inclusionary potential because, in our view, it is exclusion from the world of work which is the ultimate cause of the various other exclusions experienced by disabled people (Oliver 1990; Barnes 1991). If properly pursued, such an approach will also reduce public expenditure by taking people off social security payments and putting them into work, hence, making more people net givers to rather than takers from society.

We are not suggesting that all disabled people can work at the same pace as non-disabled people or that everyone with an impairment should work in the conventional sense. Expecting severely disabled people to be as productive as non-disabled people is one of the most oppressive aspects of capitalist society (Oliver and Barnes 1997). This will mean a reappraisal of the very meaning of work but this is something we must not shy away from. People could and should be rewarded for their contribution to the general good. Indeed, all governments provide large grants and subsidies for employers who provide work for others. As a society we recognise that employing people involves considerable skill and hard work. Personal assistance users can and often do employ as many as four or five personal assistants. Surely, the same principle applies?

In general, disabled people are fully supportive of such a strategy though it must be remembered that the majority are over 65 and, therefore, such a strategy is largely irrelevant to their needs (Martin *et al.* 1988). That being said, as far as the nearly two million disabled people of working age are concerned, if it is successful, it will succeed in taking many off welfare payments, such as incapacity benefit, for example, and out of the poverty trap. In turn, this would reduce public expenditure on state benefits which is precisely what both the government and the overwhelming majority of disabled people want.

Unfortunately, it appears likely that the government will attempt to cut social security payments before fully implementing the welfare to work programme, indicating that there is little confidence in the success of such a policy. There is no real need for such cynicism, however. As we have shown, organisations of disabled people have been arguing for many years for strong, enforceable, comprehensive anti-discrimination legislation: legislation which applies to all employers across the whole labour market and to its supporting infrastructure. Such a policy will ensure that considerable numbers of disabled people can take their rightful place in the workforce.

Moreover, the government could go even further than this if it is fully committed to getting disabled people into work. It could, for example, set targets for all government departments and state organisations to achieve in respect of employing disabled people, including organisations such as the health service, local authorities, universities and so on. In its dealings with the private sector it could also use similar targets to enforce contract compliance. Finally, it could switch the grants it gives to the voluntary sector to organisations controlled and run by disabled people whose record in employing their own puts the traditional voluntary sector to shame.

Such an integrated strategy could take hundreds of thousands of disabled people off state welfare payments and, in so doing, reduce the pressures on public expenditure and pave the way for a more equitable and just society. Lest anyone thinks such a strategy is over-simplistic or an impossible dream, it should be remembered that within a few months of the start of the Second World War, 400 000 previously unemployed disabled people were incorporated into Britain's workforce at all levels and made a significant contribution to the war effort (Humphries and Gordon 1992).

Simply cutting cash benefits to disabled people is a strategy doomed to failure for many reasons. First, similar attempts in the past have yielded only marginal savings because disability is a very difficult category to define and hence police. Additionally, cash is not only good for disabled people but the economy as a whole. For example, Motability, the organisation which provides cars for disabled people, buys more cars every year than do car rental firms such as Hertz or Avis, so stimulating the motor industry in particular and the economy as a whole. Finally, all the research evidence we have clearly demonstrates that giving disabled people cash is the best way to reduce their dependency on others and the state (Oliver and Zarb 1992; Zarb and Nadash 1994).

Also, the problem is not so much that cash benefits create dependency for disabled people, but that vast numbers of people with impairments are socialised into dependency by key components of the traditional welfare state. Special schools, day centres, residential institutions, social security payments which keep people in care, all perform this role (Barnes 1990, 1991) and all could be targeted instead of cash benefits which free people from dependency. Moreover, the vested interests of local authorities who support dependency-creating services, the special schools lobby, the alliance of the charities and the voluntary sector, all of whom are reliant on disabled people's continued dependence for their very existence, would have to be tackled too. Any government genuinely committed to creating a modern welfare state must ultimately address such services and the concerns of the vast numbers of people dependent on them for their livelihood.

We are not suggesting that the provision of essential services to disabled people should be left to the anarchy of the market or, indeed, to charity for we know from historical and contemporary analysis that in societies without a state-sponsored welfare system the lives of the vulnerable are greatly impoverished. However, a radical programme which opened up employment opportunities and removed disabling welfare barriers would be something that the disabled people's movement and governments could unite over.

Inclusionary visions for disabled people

In the post-1945 years, and particularly so in the period following the 1960s, disabled people have increasingly come together to collectivise their experiences and in the process focus on society's failure to address their needs and their systematic exclusion from the mainstream of social activity. This has inevitably centred on the welfare state and the way it is organised, as well as looking at the exclusionary practices of society as a whole. At the heart of this analysis lies the call for meaningful and realisable control of the services on which people with impairments are forced to depend, and the introduction of policies capable of creating and sustaining a society whose values and culture will accommodate all its citizens regardless of difference.

What we are proposing is a bottom-up user-led approach to welfare, building on disabled people's own experiences of the welfare state. These broadly negative experiences have led increasingly large sections of the disabled community to develop their own services at both the local and national levels. As we described in Chapter 7, these include an appropriate range of disability benefits, access and rights to all the necessary information on both impairment and disability, integrated housing schemes, user-led services located in Centres of Integrated Living (CILs) controlled by disabled people, adequately funded personal assistance schemes, a comprehensive and enforceable anti-discrimination policy applying to all aspects of life, and a properly resourced disabled people's movement. Further, as the latter is widely accepted as representing disabled people's interests, it has a legitimate place within the political institutions of the state.

All this is underpinned by a philosophy captured in the demands made by disabled people from all over the world. These include the call for meaningful and effective user led services which incorporate personal assistance services. Thus accommodating various models of independent/integrated living for disabled people; regardless of the nature or severity of their impairment. All of which must be underpinned by comprehensive and enforceable welfare legislation which ensures basic human rights for all (see Documents A, B, C, D, in Part Two).

Elsewhere (Zarb and Oliver 1993), we have described how all these elements can be integrated into what we have called the supportive environment model of state-provided welfare (see Figure 8.1).

Furthermore, in an article entitled 'Developing New Services' (1996) Vic Finkelstein and Ossie Stuart outline a similar model to this in two fundamental respects. First, there should be a rigid separation between impairment and disability-based services: what they call medical and lifestyle services (Finkelstein and Stuart 1996: 187). Second, these services must be provided on an integrated basis; experience shows that attempting to deal with complex issues one at a time is doomed to failure and simply reinforces dependency.

Finkelstein and Stuart (1996) go on to suggest that as a consequence of their proposals there will be no place for a National Health Service in their 'brave new world' precisely because it conflates medical and lifestyle needs. We are not convinced of this and, in any case, feel that the precise organisational structure of the revitalised welfare state is not something that can or should be specified in advance. This will emerge as the welfare state is transformed and needs a much broader analysis and debate because such a transformation will involve changes in services for everyone, not just disabled people.

Figure 8.1   Building a supportive environment

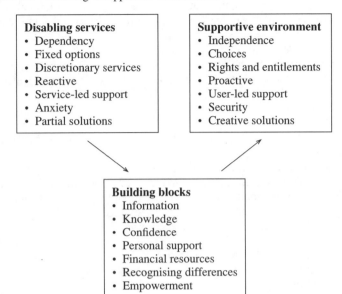

Disabling services
• Dependency
• Fixed options
• Discretionary services
• Reactive
• Service-led support
• Anxiety
• Partial solutions

Supportive environment
• Independence
• Choices
• Rights and entitlements
• Proactive
• User-led support
• Security
• Creative solutions

Building blocks
• Information
• Knowledge
• Confidence
• Personal support
• Financial resources
• Recognising differences
• Empowerment

Inclusionary visions for all

While impairments of varying kinds, both congenital and acquired, have existed and been recognised throughout recorded history and in all known cultures and societies, social responses to impairments have varied considerably. Disability, or the social oppression of people with perceived impairments, on the other hand, is a social creation. Within Western culture to be a disabled person is to be viewed as, at best, somehow less than whole and, at worst, not quite human. As a consequence, disabled people have been and continue to be treated differently from non-disabled peers. Furthermore, from the beginnings of industrialisation through to the latter half of the twentieth century this has invariably resulted in their systematic exclusion from the mainstream of community life.

This is not to suggest that disabled people are the only group to experience this form of oppression; patriarchy, classism, racism, heterosexism and ageism have each, to varying degrees, accompanied Western economic and cultural development. Biological arguments have, historically, been used to justify the differential treatment of women, working-class people, other cultures, minority ethnic groups, lesbians and gay men, and children and older people. All of this serves to endorse the fact that the experience of oppression is significantly more complex for anyone who falls within one or more of these categories but just happens to have an accredited impairment.

Furthermore, while a number of important sociopolitical movements have emerged to represent these groups and, in so doing, work for change, they have, without exception, ignored disability and its impact on those they claim to represent. Several disabled women (Fine and Asch 1985; Morris 1991; Wendell 1996), for example, have drawn attention to the fact that feminism has failed to address the needs of disabled women. As a consequence, traditional assumptions about the problem of disability remained unchallenged until the emergence of the disabled people's movement.

There are two important points to be made about this. First, while we have focused on the oppression of disabled people and the role of the welfare state in both producing and confronting that oppression, similar arguments could and, indeed, have been made about welfare and other oppressed groups (see, for example, Williams 1989). Additionally, oppression is not a simple matter; people may be oppressed on the grounds of a variety of factors such as impairment, sex, age, sexuality and so on (Morris 1991; Stuart 1992; Shakespeare *et al.* 1997).

These are matters of central importance which will have to be addressed in both theory and practice if we are to build a welfare state which is inclusive to all and not one which includes some at the expense of others. In theoretical terms Peter Leonard (1997) suggests that collective resistance to cutbacks in the welfare state might be organised around notions of the 'universal other'. For us this poses the same dilemma as the one raised by Liggett (1988) and discussed in Chapter 5; accepting the concept requires acceptance of difference based on the us/them dualism.

For us, the commonality among different groups is not otherness but the experience of oppression under capitalism. Collective resistance and, indeed, collective reconstruction, must be organised around the different ways that experience manifests itself, and a genuine desire to end our own sectional oppressions by challenging all oppression. The disabled people's movement has made a formidable start in this direction by organising a collective movement within an oppressed population which is characterised by difference in terms of impairments and degrees of impairment, gender, class, ethnicity, sexuality and age, but who are united in their opposition to disability: the disabling tendencies of modern society (Campbell and Oliver 1996).

For it is overwhelmingly obvious that a truly inclusive welfare system must embrace and accommodate the needs of all oppressed individuals and groups. It must not be predicated on false and artificially created distinctions such as those between disabled people and 'carers'. It must include all disabled children, born and unborn, whose right to life and health care must be no more and no less than that of non-disabled peers. It must include children and adults from all backgrounds and diversities of experience. All of this will help to bring about the emergence of an all-embracing culture and value system which values and celebrates the social rather than the selfish, and explores the real meaning of what it is to be human.

In pointing to the issue of being human, we have argued in this book that the impact of globalisation on other cultures and nations has meant that the economic and social forces impacting on welfare are broadly similar all over the world. Questions about the value and affordability of state welfare systems are being asked in all manner of nation states; it is only the context in which these questions are being asked that is different. Thus, in the over-resourced minority world in which we live, questions are being asked about cutting existing state welfare structures, whereas in the under-resourced majority world, questions focus on whether such structures should be established in the first place. In our view the right question is being asked but in the wrong way.

Can we afford to build a world without welfare states?

There is little doubt that in the twenty-first century, if unchecked, capitalist development has important and potentially negative implications for us all, regardless of where we live. After all, capitalism is about the unrelenting search for and the generation of ever-increasing profits. At the bottom line, there are only two ways to produce profit: one is through the exploitation of the environment, and the other is through the exploitation of humans. The consequences of the mismanagement and unregulated exploitation of the former are becoming increasingly apparent; examples include climatic change, worldwide environmental pollution, and an inescapable exhaustion of essential natural resources. Further, the globalisation of Western values and patterns of consumption is stimulating a demand among the world's population for a lifestyle which cannot be satisfied. As it is a lifestyle dependent on the continued and unequal distribution of increasingly precious resources (Harrison 1992; Independent Commission of Quality of Life 1996) serious environmental, political and social crises will almost certainly ensue. The only way that this situation might be avoided is by the gradual but systematic rejection of the market-led strategies of the past and the generation of a culture which places the needs of the many on a par with those of the few; a culture which celebrates rather than denigrates the meaning of social welfare and the state's role in the provision of that welfare.

Yet there is a growing consensus among politicians, policy-makers and the population as a whole that the traditional approach to welfare provision is both economically and politically untenable. There is mounting evidence from a variety of worldwide sources that conventional top-down professionally led services are counter-productive both in terms of resources – financial and human – and the alleviation of poverty, dependence and suffering (Hellander *et al.* 1989, 1993; Coleridge 1993; Craig and Mayo 1995; DS 1996; Taylor 1996).

As this book has shown, the disabled people's movement, against all the odds, has provided a political, cultural and practical foundation on which such a project might be constructed.

Conclusion

Although versions of the good society vary, for us it is a world in which all human beings, regardless of impairment, age, gender, social class or minority ethnic status, can coexist as equal members of the community, secure in the knowledge that their needs will be met and that their views will be recognised, respected and valued. It will be a very different world from the one in which we now live. It will be a world which is truly democratic, characterised by genuine and meaningful equality of opportunity, with far greater equity in terms of wealth and income, with enhanced choice and freedom, and with a proper regard for environmental and social continuity. The creation of such a world will be a long and difficult process.

But without a vision of how things should and ought to be, it is easy to lose your way and give up in the face of adversity and opposition. As we move into the twenty-first century, there is a growing sense of impotence among both politicians and academics. Politicians feel unable to control globalised economic forces and academics, obsessed with the collapse of modernity and the coming of postmodernity, no longer attempt to describe the world as it ought to be.

In our view, disabled people and their organisations have taken the first steps and initiated a glimpse of that vision of how the world ought to be. In fact, for us, disabled people have no choice but to attempt to build a better world because it is impossible to have a vision of inclusionary capitalism: we all need a world where impairment is valued and celebrated and all disabling barriers are eradicated. Such a world would be inclusionary for all. It is up to everyone, but especially those involved in the development and implementation of social policy – both planners and practitioners – to nurture it and help make it a reality.

PART TWO

Selected policy statements from disabled people's organisations

(A) Union of The Physically Impaired Against Segregation

Aims

The Union aims to have all segregated facilities for physically impaired people replaced by arrangements for us to participate fully in society. These arrangements must include the necessary financial, medical, technical, educational and other help required from the State to enable us to gain the maximum possible independence in daily living activities, to achieve mobility, to undertake productive work, and to live where and how we choose with full control over our lives.

Policy statement

1. Disability and segregation
Britain today has the necessary knowledge and the advanced technology to bring physically impaired people into the mainstream of life and enable us to contribute fully to society. But instead of the country's resources being concentrated on basic human problems like ours, they are frequently mis-spent, for example, on making sophisticated weapons of destruction, and on projects like Concorde and Centre Point. So despite the creation today of such an enormous capacity, which could help overcome disability, the way this capacity is misdirected means that many physically impaired people are still unnecessarily barred from full participation in society. We find ourselves isolated and excluded by such things as flights of steps, inadequate public and personal transport, unsuitable housing, rigid work routines in factories and offices, and a lack of up-to-date aids and equipment.

2. There are a few individual examples of severely impaired people being able to overcome many of these barriers by the use of sufficient resources in the right way. They prove that integration is possible. But as a group we are still often forced to put up with segregated and inferior facilities. We get sent to special schools, colleges or training centres. We are systematically channelled into segregated factories, centres, homes, hostels and clubs. If we do manage to become mobile, it is often in antiquated tricycles or specially labelled transport. All these segregated forms of help represented progress in years past. But since

the means for integration now undoubtedly exists, our confinement to segregated facilities is increasingly oppressive and dehumanising.

3. Recent advances

The struggles of disabled people and their relatives and friends, together with advances in technology and medical science, have it is true resulted in larger numbers of us participating more fully in ordinary society in recent years. Some of the barriers which segregate us have been partially overcome or dismantled. So a good proportion of people with paraplegia, or those who are blind, for example, have become able to work and to lead relatively active lives which would have been hard to imagine less than 50 years ago. These developments have meant a positive shift in the attitudes of some able-bodied people as they have responded to our presence amongst them.

4. Such advances show that general attitudes can be changed for the better. They also point to our increased participation in society as the principal means for achieving further change. But they cannot blind us to what remains the basic reality of the position of disabled people as a group. This society is based on the necessity for people to compete in the labour market in order to earn a living. To the employer of labour, the physically impaired are not usually as good a buy as the non-impaired. We therefore end up at or near the bottom of this society as an oppressed group.

5. Low bargaining power

When we do succeed in getting employment, our comparatively low productivity means that we have low bargaining-power when it comes to negotiating decent treatment and facilities. Our position is similar to that of many people who are middle-aged or elderly, who have had break-downs, or are 'mentally handicapped', black, ex-prisoners, unskilled workers, etc. We are usually among the first to lose our jobs and be cast on the scrap-heap when it suits the 'needs' of the economy. If we are lucky we may be drawn in again, to do the worst paid work, when business starts to boom once more. If we are unlucky, then we could face a lifetime on the degrading, means-tested poverty line. If we are very unlucky we may be consigned to a soul-destroying institution.

6. Institutions – the ultimate human scrap heaps

The Union of the Physically Impaired believes that the reality of our position as an oppressed group can be seen most clearly in segregated residential institutions, the ultimate human scrap-heaps of this society. Thousands of people, whose only crime is being physically impaired, are sentenced to these prisons for life – which may these days be a long one. For the vast majority there is still no alternative, no appeal, no remission of sentence for good behaviour, no escape except the escape from life itself.

7. The cruelty, petty humiliation, and physical and mental deprivation suffered in residential institutions, where isolation and segregation have been carried to extremes, lays bare the essentially oppressive relations of this society with its physically impaired members. As in most similar places, such as special schools, there are some staff and volunteers doing their best to help the residents. But their efforts are systematically overwhelmed by the basic function of segregated institutions, which is to look after batches of disabled people – and in the process convince them that they cannot realistically expect to participate fully in society and earn a good living. This function was generally appropriate when special residential institutions first came into being, since in the competitive conditions of the time many physically impaired people could not even survive without their help. But now it has become increasingly possible for severely impaired people not just to survive, but also to work and become fully integrated, the need for segregated institutions no longer exists in the way it did. They have become seriously out of step with the changed social and technological conditions of Britain today.

8. Support for residential struggles

The Union of the Physically Impaired regards the neglected issues of institutions as of crucial importance in the field of disability. We therefore place great emphasis on supporting the struggles of residents in existing residential institutions for better conditions, for full control over their personal affairs, and for a democratic say in the management of their home, centre or unit. The Union strongly opposes all attempts by the authorities to impose restrictions on visiting; to fix times for getting into and out of bed; to limit residents' freedom to come in and go out when they wish; to enforce medical and nursing opinions, or to transfer residents to other institutions against their will.

9. The Union sees a need for a charter which will focus on basic rights often denied when people are dependent on others for personal needs. Disabled people living in institutions will be offered help if they wish to organise locally in defence of their rights. The Union will develop an advice and mutual-help service to assist with negotiations, formation of residents' committees etc. When asked, we will mobilise support and publicity on a national basis for those involved in particular struggles.

10. Alternatives needed

The Union is opposed to the building of any further segregated institutions by the State or by voluntary organisations. We believe that providing adequate services to people in their own homes is a much better use of resources. We also call urgently for the provision of non-institutional alternative housing, for example, along the lines of the Fokus scheme in Sweden, which makes genuine progress towards secure, integrated, and active living for disabled people who need extensive personal help. The Union will try to assist anyone who seeks to move out – or stay out – of an institution. But we fully respect the feelings of individuals who regard institutional life as their best solution at the present time. We understand also that some disabled people will disagree with our views on segregation, and we hope that they will organise to put forward their arguments too.

11. Real change

The Union's eventual object is to achieve a situation where as physically impaired people we all have the means to choose where and how we wish to live. This will involve the phasing out of segregated institutions maintained by the State or charities. While many of these institutions are maintained at a huge cost, it is inconceivable that we will all receive in addition the full resources needed to provide us with a genuine opportunity to live as we choose. This point applies not just to residential homes, hospital units, hostels, villages and settlements, but also to other kinds of segregated facilities. As long as there are vastly expensive special schools, colleges and day-centres, heavily subsidised workshops and factories, and separate holiday camps and hotels, there can be no question of sufficient alternative provision being made to ensure that we all have a real opportunity of equal participation in normal educational, work and leisure activities.

12. Disablement outside institutions

Our Union maintains that the present existence of segregated institutions and facilities is of direct relevance even for less severely impaired people who may expect to avoid having to use them. Those of us who live outside institutions can fully understand the meaning of disability in this society only when we take account of what happens to the people who come at the bottom of our particular group. Their existence and their struggles are an essential part of the reality of disability and to ignore them is like assessing the condition of elderly people in this society without considering the existence of geriatric wards.

13. It is also true that the kind of prejudiced attitudes we all experience – other people being asked if we take sugar in our tea is the usual example – are related to the continued unnecessary existence of sheltered institutions. Those who patronise us are indicating that they think we are not capable of participating fully and making our own decisions. They are harking back to the time when disabled people had to be sheltered much more, and they imply that really we ought to be back in our rightful place – that is, a special school, club, hospital unit, home or workshop. Physically impaired people will never be fully accepted in ordinary society while segregated institutions continue to exist, if only because their unnecessary survival today reinforces out of date attitudes and prejudices.

14. Medical tradition

Both inside and outside institutions, the traditional way of dealing with disabled people has been for doctors and other professionals to decide what is best for us. It is of course a fact that we sometimes require skilled medical help to treat our physical impairments – operations, drugs and nursing care. We may also need therapists to help restore or maintain physical function, and to advise us on aids to independence and mobility. But the imposition of medical authority, and of a medical definition of our problems of living in society, have to be resisted strongly. First and foremost we are people, not 'patients', 'cases', 'spastics', 'the deaf', 'the blind', 'wheelchairs' or 'the sick'. Our Union rejects entirely any idea of medical or other experts having the right to tell us how we should live, or withholding information from us, or take decisions behind our backs.

15. We reject also the whole idea of 'experts' and professionals holding forth on how we should accept our disabilities, or giving learned lectures about the 'psychology' of disablement. We already know what it feels like to be poor, isolated, segregated, done good to, stared at, and talked down to – far better than any able-bodied expert. We as a Union are not interested in descriptions of how awful it is to be disabled. What we are interested in, are ways of changing our conditions of life, and thus overcoming the disabilities which are imposed on top of our physical impairments by the way this society is organised to exclude us. In our view, it is only the actual impairment which we must accept; the additional and totally unnecessary problems caused by the way we are treated are essentially to be overcome and not accepted. We look forward to the day when the army of 'experts' on our social and psychological problems can find more productive work.

16. The right kind of help

We know that as a small, weak, minority group, disabled people cannot achieve a fully human life by their own efforts alone. We need and welcome the help of sympathetic able-bodied people. But the basic problem we face is our exclusion from full social participation. It follows that this oppressive situation can be put right only by disabled people actually taking a more active part in society. The efforts of professionals and other able-bodied people are therefore really constructive only when they build on and encourage the self-help and activity of disabled people themselves. This is why our energies as a Union will be directed mainly towards discussion and common action with other disabled people. Neither we as a Union, nor able-bodied people, can solve other disabled people's problems for them. Those problems will be correctly tackled precisely to the extent that we all as disabled people become involved and active in our own rehabilitation.

17. The need for a union

Disabled people everywhere are already struggling against their isolation, segregation and other forms of oppression. Every day each of us has to face our own individual problems. And we are now increasingly getting together in groups to tackle more effectively the problems we find we have in common. This is shown by the vast growth of disability organisations in the last 25 years in Britain. Our Union takes this process of coming together a stage further. We are not restricted to one aspect of physical disability (e.g. mobility or incomes), nor to people with one medical diagnosis, nor to those in one locality. The Union exists simply to offer help to all physically impaired people in the fight to change the conditions of life which oppress us and to realise our full human potential.

18. Action

Various kinds of action in support of disabled people's struggles will be undertaken by the Union as resources become available. Apart from publishing pamphlets and an open newsletter, we will mount action campaigns on various issues. We will build up information and advice services, and organise financial, secretarial and other forms of practical assistance. For example, individuals may ask for help in fighting bureaucratic delays and efficiency, or a refusal to provide equipment, aids or other kinds of service. Other people may want assistance in tackling organisations about the provision of ramps or lifts in buildings. Residents in institutions may seek help and national publicity if they are victimised by the authorities. People in sheltered workshops or centres may ask our support in their struggles to improve their appalling rates of pay. The Union will succeed only when it helps to achieve real benefits and improved conditions for disabled people.

19. Guidelines for action

But our actions will become more effective if we make sure that we also learn from the practical struggles which take place. So an essential part of the Union's task is to develop increasingly clear guidelines for further action. We will not do this by careful discussion about what we and other disabled people are doing, and about the real nature of the problems we face at a particular time. We need to learn from our failures and successes, and so develop arguments and a theory which have been proved to work – because they do actually bring about practical gains for disabled people. In this way the value of our practical experience will be multiplied many times over, as the essential lessons learned from it are made available to other disabled people now and in the future.

20. Terms of membership

Full membership of the Union is open to residents of Britain who are significantly physically impaired and who accept the Policies and Constitution. Full members are expected to take some active part in Union affairs, since the Union is firmly based on the conviction that as disabled people we can only make real progress through actively struggling for change. Members will of course have different capacities at different times, and 'active' here means at least some involvement in discussion of policy. We are sympathetic to the fact that some potential members may have problems of communication, and the Union will give encouragement and help in these circumstances. However, disabled people who feel they cannot at present contribute in this way may keep in touch by subscribing to our open Newsletter.

21. Able-bodied people who agree with the Union Policies and Constitution can become associate members. Associate members may receive the internal circular, the open newsletter and other publications, and may take part in meetings, discussions and other events. But they are not entitled to vote on Union affairs, nor may they hold any Union office. Genuine supporters will recognise the need for us to control our own Union and so develop our powers of decision, organisation and action. They will understand too, that since we experience daily the actual reality of disability, we are less likely than able-bodied people to be deceived about the true nature of our oppression and the radical changes necessary to overcome it.

22. Other oppression groups
The particular forms which oppression takes in this society differ somewhat for each distinct oppressed group. Some, such as people who are called 'mentally handicapped', or those 'mentally ill', clearly have a great deal in common with us. Full membership of our Union is however based simply on the fact of physical impairment. This is because we believe the important thing at the moment is to clarify the facts of our situation and the problems associated with physical impairment. But it is fundamental to our approach that we will seek to work with other oppressed groups and support their struggles to achieve a decent life. What all oppressed people share is a vital interest in changing society to overcome oppression, and the Union is therefore anxious to join in common action to achieve such change.

23. Democratic control
Democratic control of the Union rests with all full members, and policy is decided on a majority basis after thorough discussion in a confidential circular or at general meetings. Full discussion of policy by members is necessary if we are continually to develop our action and thinking along the right lines. But once decisions have been made, members undertake not to oppose them publicly while they wish to remain in the Union. Both elements in this combination are regarded as essential for genuine progress – thorough internal discussion by members, together with a refusal to indulge in public criticism of Union policies.

24. Day-to-day decisions on Union affairs are in the hands of an Executive Committee, elected by, and responsible to, all full members. The Executive Committee holds the Union's funds. It arranges for the production of the internal circular, the regular open newsletter, and of

occasional pamphlets and other publications. The Committee also speaks and acts officially for the Union on the basis of agreed policy. The overall task of the Committee within the Union is to facilitate the active participation and development of all members.

25. *Special interest groups*
Special-interest groups within the Union will be formed by members concerned with a particular aspect of disability. Examples may include residents' rights in institutions, incomes, employment, special education, provision of aids and equipment, housing alternatives in Britain and overseas, medical and technical research, rehabilitation. Within the general principles of the Union these groups will work out actions and ideas based on their special interests and experiences. Reports by them on particular topics will be published in the name of the Union from time to time.

26. *Finance*
All registered charities receive valuable tax concessions, but they are not allowed to campaign directly for political change. We regard political involvement as essential if disabled people are ever to make real advances. So in order to protect our independence of action we are not registered with the Charity Commissioners. Nor do we intend to appeal for funds publicly in the name of the Union. We believe the time has come for an organisation in the disability field which does not depend heavily on public fund-raising. We shall be free to speak and act on the basis of Union members' views rather than those of financial supporters and noble patrons. Union expenses will be met by subscription, by donations, and by such means as the sale of literature.

27. *Other disability organisations*
The Union aims to ensure that all the organisations concerned with disability become fully democratic and responsive to the real needs and wishes of disabled people. We therefore seek a much greater say in all the organisations which affect our lives, both by Union members as individuals and by other disabled people. Any official Union representatives appointed to committees of other groups will promote Union policies and report back regularly to members. In addition, the Union will keep a watchful, independent eye on the policies and practice of all disability organisations. We will try not to duplicate effort, and will welcome constructive comment and help from other groups. We will ourselves offer support and co-operation whenever possible. But the Union will not hesitate to speak out freely, and act independently, when we believe the interests of disabled people require it. It will be for disabled people as a whole to judge whether or not we are correct.

Adopted: 3 December 1974
Amended: 9 August 1976

(B) Liberation Policy of People with Disabilities

2nd draft 1981

1. All human beings have an equal right to live, to eat adequately, to housing, to clean water, to a basic standard of health and hygiene, to privacy, to education, to work, to marry (or not), have children (or not), to determine their own sexuality, to state an opinion, to participate in decisions which affect their lives, to share fully in the social life of their community and to contribute to the well-being of others to the full extent of their capabilities.
2. At the present time only a few, a privileged section of the world's population, enjoy all these rights, whilst the majority of people are divided into groups which are comparatively underprivileged. The basis of the division is economic. Most of these groups are sub-divided (e.g. women into black, brown, white, yellow, young, old, married, single, Jewish, gay, working-class) until each group experiences itself as a powerless minority.
3. Whilst the basis of the division is economic, the power to sustain the situation is primarily of a psychological nature. Information is given by way of stereotyping, incorrect or biased histories, demonstrations of violence against minority groups (e.g. the Holocaust) and numerous other ways that persuade the members of both the privileged and under-privileged that they deserve their position in society. It is the personal belief in that idea that allows each person and each group to accept their condition.
4. People with disabilities are one such group, but have two special features:
   (a) It is a group whose members embrace every other group.
   (b) The cause of the special title, unlike most other classifications (e.g. black) is often an additional drain on the resources of the individual, i.e. it is not inherently distressing to be black, whilst it may be to suffer from painful arthritis.
5. Taking our special features into account, a draft policy for liberation should include the following:
   - To reach out and make contact with our members in every societal group.
   - To learn to recognise the affects of society's conditioning on people with disabilities, and to create ways in which people's awareness can be heightened to a point where their self-image changes from a negative to a positive one, from weak to strong.
   - To recognise that the division of people with disabilities on the grounds of different disabilities (paralysed, deaf, people with visual handicaps, epileptic etc.) has been divisive, and one of the major factors in our slowness to join together to change our common difficulties.
   - To learn about each other's disabilities in order to be informed and able to support each other over genuine difficulties.
   - To seek to abolish all forms of segregation particularly in educational settings and residential institutions.
   - To seek allies amongst able-bodied people (i.e. people who will help us to fight for ourselves – not on our behalf).
   - To seek complete self-determination and control over our representation in the media (TV, books, films, adverts, etc.) and to have control over information put out about us.
   - To seek to unite organisations and institutions representing people with disabilities to fight for a common policy of liberation. (This does not mean detracting organisations from their original aims e.g. medical research, if these aims are complementary to the movement.)

- To work out a just economic policy taking into account that with industrialised countries in particular, a disability can require extra income to allow the person to reach the same standard of living as able-bodied people, whilst at the same time the competitive nature of earning money can exclude people with a certain degree of disability from making an equal contribution to work.
- To inform as many people with disabilities as possible of their rights, in particular those included in the United Nations Declaration of Human Rights for Disabled Persons.
- To encourage people with disabilities to organise themselves into active groups which will discuss the implications of achieving their rights at international, national, and local levels, and will seek to change or influence conditions around them accordingly.
- To make allies of, and be allies to, all other oppressed groups.

Source: *In From the Cold: A Liberation Magazine for People with Disabilities*, first issue, June 1981, pp. 19–20.

(C) Disabled People's International

(Extracts from 'Proceedings of the First World Congress of Disabled People's International', Singapore, 30 November–4 December 1981)

Fundamental values

We maintain that all people are of equal value. This conviction implies that disabled people have the right to participate in every sphere of society. All technical and practical means available should be utilised to facilitate the participation of the disabled in the various forms of service and social activities of our societies.

The principal of equal value implies that the needs of each and every individual are of equal importance, that their needs must be made the basis for the planning of our societies and that all available resources be employed in such a way as to ensure equal participation for each and every individual. Disabled policies, therefore, very often concern the distribution of resources in the society and are, more often than not, political issues.

As a consequence of this philosophy, every development scheme or programme must contain measures which lead to the participation of the disabled. In measures for the disabled in fields where services and other activities are made available on a commercial basis, society must safeguard the interests of the disabled in order to ensure that they are not excluded from these services and activities. Anyone responsible for a particular area of activity also has primary responsibility for making the particular activity and accessible to the disabled. The supreme decision making body in society has ultimate responsibility for the position of the disabled.

Disabled people have a right to grow up in their natural environment. We therefore reject all forms of segregation, and we refuse to accept lifetime isolation in special institutions.

Basic rights

In our common endeavour for full participation and equality for the world's disabled, the following rights are of fundamental importance.

The right to education

Knowledge is the basis for all development. Every child has the right to education, and this right must consequently include all disabled children. In the initial stages of all development schemes in the educational field the needs of the disabled must be taken into account. Teaching should be carried out in the child's natural environment. Any steps necessary to make the teaching process available and meaningful should become a normal part of the work carried out in schools.

The right to rehabilitation

Anyone afflicted by any form of disability must be guaranteed the opportunity for training, information, and education which aims to or compensate for the functional disability. We regard such rehabilitation as both a right and an obligation for the disabled individual.

The right to employment

Employment is the basis for all personal and shared prosperity. The right to gainful employment must be extended to include the disabled. The obvious discrimination of the disabled in the labour market must be substituted for by opportunities, so that each and every individual, according to ability and capacity, can work and contribute to the maintenance of themselves and family.

The right to economic security

No human being should be obliged to beg for a living. The primary aim of any society should be to provide employment opportunities for all groups including the disabled. In cases where this aim cannot be realised society must provide for basic economic security in the form of unemployment benefits and pensions.

The right to independent living

Everyone has a right to a home of their own, that is a dwelling which provides opportunities for independent living and which allows for the maintenance of personal integrity. Measures such as special services and adjustments to the physical surroundings are necessary if this right is to include all groups of disabled people.

The right to participate in social and cultural activities

In such areas as recreation, association activities and other cultural activities there are a multitude of obstacles which prevent participation by the disabled. These obstacles must be eliminated and opportunities made available for the disabled to participate in the various cultural and social activities on equal terms with the rest of society.

The right to influence

Each and every individual must be guaranteed equal democratic opportunity to influence the shaping of society. For the disabled there are innumerable obstacles to full participation in the political process of decision making. The right to information must be guaranteed for groups with varying communication difficulties. Public premises must be made accessible to the disabled. The disabled must also be given the opportunity to participate in debates and meetings. Furthermore, organisations of the disabled must be given decisive influence in regard to all measures on their behalf.

The right to equal partners

Disabled people have the right to equal participation in the decision making processes of all policies services, and programmes that effect their lives.

(D) European Network for Independent Living

European Conference on Personal Assistance Services for Disabled People organised by the international disability movement with the help of GRAEL in the Rainbow Group in the European Parliament and the GRUNEN in the German Bundestag.

We, more than a hundred disabled people from Netherlands, United Kingdom, Denmark, Italy, Switzerland, Sweden, France Austria, Finland, Belgium, USA, Hungary, FRG, and Norway, have come together from April 12th to 14th at Strasbourg in France to raise the issue of personal assistance services as a pre-requisite for independent living for disabled people.

In our view, independence is not measured by the quantities of tasks one can perform without assistance, but the quality of life one can have with assistance. Assistance in the context of independent living is given within the framework of a civil right and a service under the control of the recipient – where, when, how and by whom. Today these services are not being realised in any quantity in the European community.

Our coming together here in Strasbourg is the result of growing disability movements in countries all over the world. Increasingly we, disabled people, are raising our voices to speak against the warehousing of disabled people in special institutions, and against the denial of basic equal rights for disabled people by medical experts, policy makers and administrative officials.

In sharing our experiences about the social welfare systems and laws in our respective countries, we have found that by the exclusion of disabled people from the mainstream of society and the denial of access to personal assistance services we are prevented from entering the workforces and other spheres of social life. We are denied the right to independent living. These denials are also the basic sources of discrimination against disabled people.

We demand social welfare systems that include personal assistance services that are consumer controlled and which allow for various models of independent living for disabled people, regardless of impairment and income. We demand social welfare legislation which recognises these services as basic civil rights and which provide necessary appeal procedures. This conference is proof of a growing disability movement that will not stop until independent living and full participation in society are realised for all disabled people.

Resolutions

1. Personal assistance services are a human and civil right which must be provided at no cost to the user. These services shall serve people with all types of impairments and all ages on the basis of functional need, irrespective of personal wealth, income, marital and family status.
2. Personal assistance users shall be able to choose from a variety of personal assistance service models which together offer the choice of various degrees of user control.
3. Services shall enable the user to participate in every aspect of life such as home, work, school, leisure, travel and political life etc. These services shall enable disabled people, if they so choose, to build up a personal and family life and fulfil all the responsibilities connected with this.
4. These services must be available long term for anything up to 24 hours a day, seven days a week, and similarly on a short term or emergency basis. These services shall include assistance with personal bodily functions, communication, household, mobility, work and other related needs. In the assessment of need the consumer's view must be paramount.
5. The funding authority shall ensure that sufficient funds are available to the user for adequate support, counselling, training of the user and the assistant, if deemed necessary to the user.
6. Funding must include assistant's competitive wages and employment benefits, all legal and union required benefits, or services.
7. Funding shall be a legislative right and payment must be guaranteed regardless of funding source or local government arrangements. Funding shall not be treated as disposable/taxable income and shall not make the user ineligible for other statutory benefits or services.

8. The user should be free to appoint as personal assistants whoever they choose including family members.
9. No individual shall be placed in an institutional setting because of lack of resources, high costs, sub-standard or non-existent services.
10. There shall be a uniform judicial appeals procedure which is independent of funders, providers and assessors; is effected within a reasonable amount of time and enables the claimant to receive legal aid at the expense of the statutory authority.
11. In furtherance of all the above, disabled people and organisations controlled by them must be decisively involved at all levels of policy making including planning, implementation and development.

European Conference on Personal Assistance Services for Disabled People, 12–14 April 1989, Strasbourg, France.

Selected international charters

(E) United Nations Declaration on the Rights of Mentally Retarded Persons (UN General Assembly Resolution 28/56 Adopted 20 December 1971)

The General Assembly

Mindful of the pledge of the Member States of the United Nations under the Charter to take joint and separate action in co-operation with the Organisation to promote higher standards of living, full employment and conditions of economic and social progress and development.

Reaffirming faith in human rights and fundamental freedoms and in the principles of peace, of the dignity and worth of the human person and of social justice proclaimed in the Charter.

Recalling the principles of the Universal Declaration of Human rights, the International Convenants on Human Rights, the Declaration of the Rights of the Child and the standards already set for social progress in the constitutions, conventions, recommendations and resolutions of the International Labour Organisation, the United Nations Educational, Scientific and Cultural Organisation, the World Health Organisation, the United Nations Children's Fund and other organisations concerned.

Emphasising that the Declaration on Social Progress and Development has proclaimed the necessity of protecting the rights and assuring the welfare and rehabilitation of the physically and mentally disadvantaged.

Bearing in mind the necessity of assisting mentally retarded persons to develop their abilities in various fields of activities and of promoting their integration as far as possible in normal life.

Aware that certain countries, at their present stage of development, can devote only limited efforts to this end.

Proclaims this Declaration on the Rights of Mentally Retarded Persons and calls for national and international action to ensure that it will be used as a common basis and frame of reference for the protection of these rights:

1. The mentally retarded person has, to the maximum degree of feasibility, the same rights as other human beings.
2. The mentally retarded person has a right to proper medical care and physical therapy and to such education, training and rehabilitation and guidance as will enable him to develop his ability and maximum potential.
3. The mentally retarded person has a right to economic security and to a decent standard of living. He has the right to perform production work or to

engage in any other meaningful occupation to the fullest possible extent of his capabilities.

4. Whenever possible, the mentally retarded person should live with his own family or with foster parents and participate in different forms of community life. The family with which he lives should receive assistance. If care in an institution becomes necessary, it should be provided in surroundings and other circumstances as close as possible to those of normal life.

5. The mentally retarded person has a right to a qualified guardian when this is required to protect his personal well-being and interests.

6. The mentally retarded person has a right to protection from exploitation, abuse and degrading treatment. If prosecuted for any offence, he shall have a right to due process of law with full recognition being given to his degree of mental responsibility.

7. Whenever mentally retarded persons are unable, because of the severity of their handicap, to exercise all their rights in a meaningful way or it should become necessary to restrict or deny some or all of these rights, the procedure used for that restriction or denial of rights must contain proper legal safeguards against every form of abuse. This procedure must be based on an evaluation of the social capability of the mentally retarded person by qualified experts and must be subject to period review and to the right of appeal to higher authorities.

(F) United Nations Declaration on the Rights of Disabled Persons (UN General Assembly Resolution 34/47 Adopted 9 December 1975)

The General Assembly

Mindful of the pledge made by Member States, under the Charter of the United Nations, to take joint and separate action in co-operation with the Organisation to promote higher standards of living, full employment and conditions of economic and social progress and development.

Reaffirming its faith in human rights and fundamental freedoms and in the principles of peace, of the dignity and worth of the human person and of social justice proclaimed in the Charter.

Recalling the principles of the Universal Declaration of Human Rights, the International Covenants on Human Rights, the Declaration of the Rights of the Child and the Declaration on the Rights of Mentally Retarded Persons, as well as the Standards already set for social progress in the constitutions, conventions, recommendations and resolutions of the International Labour Organisation, the United Nations Educational, Scientific and Cultural Organisation, the World Health Organisation, the United Nations Children's Fund and other organisations concerned.

Recalling also Economic and Social Council resolution 1921 (LVIII) of 6 May 1975 on the prevention of disability and the rehabilitation of disabled persons.

Emphasising that the Declaration on Social Progress and Development has proclaimed the necessity of protecting the rights and assuring the welfare and rehabilitation of the physically and mentally disadvantaged.

Bearing in mind the necessity of preventing physical and mental disabilities and of assisting disabled persons to develop their abilities in the most varied fields of activities and of promoting their integration as far as possible in normal life.

Aware that certain countries, at their present stage of development, can devote only limited efforts to this end.

Proclaims this Declaration on the Rights of Disabled Persons and calls for national and international action to ensure that it will be used as a common basis and frame of reference for the protection of these rights:

1. The term 'disabled person' means any person unable to ensure by himself or herself, wholly or partly, the necessities of a normal individual and/or social life, as a result of a deficiency, either congenital or not, in his or her physical or mental capacities.
2. Disabled persons shall enjoy all the rights set forth in this Declaration. These rights shall be granted to all disabled persons without any exception whatsoever and without distinction or discrimination on the basis of race, colour, sex, language, religion, political or other opinions, national or social origin, state of wealth, birth or any other situation applying either to the disabled person himself or herself or to his or her family.
3. Disabled persons have the inherent right to respect for their human dignity. Disabled persons, whatever the origin, nature and seriousness of their handicaps and disabilities, have the same fundamental rights as their fellow-citizens of the same age, which implies first and foremost the right to enjoy a decent life, as normal and full as possible.
4. Disabled persons have the same civil and political rights as other human beings: paragraph 7 of the Declaration on the Rights of Mentally Retarded Persons applies to any possible limitation or suppression of those rights for mentally disabled persons.
5. Disabled persons are entitled to the measures designed to enable them to become as self-reliant as possible.
6. Disabled persons have the right to medical, psychological and functional treatment, including prosthetic and orthotic appliances, to medical and social rehabilitation, education, vocational training and rehabilitation, aid, counselling, placement services and other services which will enable them to develop their capabilities and skills to the maximum and will hasten the process of their social integration or reintegration.
7. Disabled persons have the right to economic and social security and to a decent level of living. They have the right, according to their capabilities, to secure and retain employment or to engage in a useful, productive and remunerative occupation and to join trade unions.
8. Disabled persons are entitled to have their special needs taken into consideration at all stages of economic and social planning.
9. Disabled persons have the right to live with their families or with foster parents and to participate in all social, creative and recreational activities. No disabled person shall be subjected, as far as his or her residence is concerned, to differential treatment other than that required by his or her condition or by the improvement which he or she may derive therefrom. If the stay of disabled person in a specialised establishment is indispensable, the environment and living conditions therein shall be as close as possible to those of the normal life of a person of his or her age.

10. Disabled persons shall be protected against all exploitation, all regulations and all treatment of a discriminatory, abusive or degrading nature.
11. Disabled persons shall be able to avail themselves of qualified legal aid when such aid proves indispensable for the protection of their persons and property. If judicial proceedings are instituted against them, the legal procedure applied shall take their physical and mental condition fully into account.
12. Organisations of disabled persons may be usefully consulted in all matters regarding the rights of disabled persons.
13. Disabled persons, their families and communities shall be fully informed, by all appropriate means, of the rights contained in this Declaration.

(G) The United Nations World Programme of Action Concerning Disabled Persons

The World Programme of Action concerning Disabled Persons (WPA) became the UN's policy document on disability in 1983 (Resolution 37/52). It recommends ways to bring about the aims of the Decade of Disabled Persons – the full and equal participation of disabled people in society. The WPA contains guidelines, looks at the situation of disabled people around the world, and recommends action at the national, regional and international levels.

It says that: 'The purpose of the World Programme of Action concerning Disabled Persons is to promote effective measures for prevention of disability, rehabilitation and the realisation of the goals of "full participation" of disabled persons in social life and development, and of "equality". This means opportunities equal to those of the whole population and an equal share in the improvement in living conditions resulting from social and economic development. These concepts should apply with the same scope and with the same urgency to all countries, regardless of their level of development.' (Paragraph 1)

The main aims of the WPA are prevention, rehabilitation and equalisation of opportunities.

Societies and governments must take action to:

(a) prevent or reduce the effects of mental, physical or sensory impairments
(b) help people with impairments to do as much as possible, through rehabilitation, aids and appliances
(c) make sure that disabled people can find out about and take part in the same activities as everyone else and can use the same services – such as transport, education and training, employment, social security, religion and entertainment
(d) consult with organisations of disabled people on the policies and programmes that directly effect them.

The WPA points out that there are more than 500 million people in the world who have physical, intellectual or sensory impairments, and that these people should have the same rights and opportunities as all other human beings.

It stresses that 'the ultimate responsibility for remedying the conditions that lead to impairment and for dealing with the consequences of disability rests with governments'.

Governments should provide services to make sure that disabled people are included in every area of economic, social and political life. The WPA has policy aims and guidelines for programmes for disabled people at the national, regional and international levels.

It also encourages the development of disabled people's organisations and says that they should be consulted in policy-making.

Extracts

Paragraph 21: A person is disabled when denied the opportunities generally available in the community that are necessary for the fundamental elements of living, including family life, education, employment, housing, financial and personal security, participation in social and political groups, religious activity, intimate and sexual relations, access to public facilities, freedom of movement and a general style of daily living.

Paragraph 71: Full participation in the basic units of society – family, social groups and community – is the essence of human experience. The right to equality of opportunity for such participation is set forth in the Universal Declaration of Human Rights and should apply to all people, including those with disabilities. In reality, however, disabled persons are often denied the opportunities of full participation in the activities of the socio-cultural system of which they are a part. This deprivation comes about through physical and social barriers that have evolved from ignorance, indifference and fear.

Paragraph 76: Many disabled persons are excluded from active participation in society because of doorways that are too narrow for wheelchairs; steps that cannot be mounted leading to buildings, buses, trains and aircraft; telephones and light switches that cannot be reached; sanitary facilities that cannot be used. Similarly, they can be excluded by other types of barriers, for example oral communication which ignores the needs of the hearing impaired and written information which ignores the needs of the visually impaired. Such barriers are the result of ignorance and lack of concern; they exist despite the fact that most of them could be avoided at no great cost by careful planning. Although some countries have enacted legislation and launched campaigns of public education to eliminate such obstacles, the problem remains a crucial one.

Paragraph 89: Matters concerning disabled persons should be treated within the appropriate general context and not separately. Each ministry or other body within the public or private sector responsible for, or working within, a specific sector should be responsible for those matters related to disabled persons which fall within its area of competence. Governments should establish a focal point (for example, a national commission, committee or similar body) to look into and follow the activities related to the World Programme of Action of various ministries, of other government agencies and of non-governmental organisations. Any mechanism set up should involve all parties concerned, including organisations of disabled persons. The body should have access to decision-makers at the highest level.

Paragraph 91: Member States should increase their assistance to organisations of disabled persons and help them organise and coordinate the representation of the interests and concerns of disabled persons.

Paragraph 92: Member States should actively seek out and encourage in every possible way the development of organisations composed of or representing disabled persons. Such organisations, in whose membership and governing bodies disabled persons, or in some cases relatives, have a decisive influence, exist in many countries. Many of them have not the means to assert themselves and fight for their rights.

Paragraph 93: Member States should establish direct contacts with such organisations and provide channels for them to influence government policies and decisions in all areas that concern them. Member States should give the necessary financial support to organisations of disabled persons for this purpose.

Paragraph 110: In drafting national human rights legislation, and with respect to national committees or similar coordinating national bodies dealing with the problems of disability, particular attention should be given to conditions which may adversely affect the ability of disabled persons to exercise the rights and freedoms guaranteed to their fellow citizens.

Paragraph 111: Member States should give attention to specific rights, such as the rights to education, work, social security and protection from inhuman or degrading treatment, and should examine these rights from the perspective of disabled persons.

Source: The Information Kit on the United Nations Standard Rules on the Equalisation of Opportunities for Persons with Disabilities by Disability Awareness in Action (DAA) 11 Belgrave Road, London SW1V 1RB. (DAA is an international information project for disabled people and their organisations run by disabled people.)

(H) Resolution of the European Disabled People's Parliament, 3 December 1993

The European Disabled People's Parliament,

(A) Recognising that disability is a human rights issue
(B) Recalling that all human rights and fundamental freedoms are universal and thus unreservedly include disabled people

(C) Bearing in mind that every person is born equal and has the same rights to life and welfare, education, living independently, equal opportunities for employment, and active participation in all aspects of society

(D) Recognising that disabled people have the right to full and equal participation in the economic and social development of Europe

(E) Considering that any direct discrimination or other negative discriminatory treatment of a disabled person is a violation of his or her rights

(F) Convinced that disabled people should be guaranteed equal opportunity through the elimination of all socially-determined barriers, be they physical, financial, social or psychological, which exclude or restrict full participation in society

(G) Realising that disabled people face three forms of unfair discrimination – direct discrimination, indirect discrimination, and 'unequal burdens' imposed by socially constructed barriers

(H) Having regard to the World Programme of Action concerning Disabled Persons adopted by the United Nations' General Assembly at its thirty-seventh session

(J) Convinced that disabled people, through their representative organisations, have the right to be consulted on issues and decisions affecting their human rights

1. Invites the Community institutions and the Member States of the European Community to take practical steps to guarantee the human rights of disabled people by the adoption or adjustment of legally binding instruments, and to adopt and to ensure implementation of the UN Standard Rules on the Equalisation of Opportunities for disabled people.

2. Invites the Commission of the European Communities:

   (i) to examine the status of equal opportunities within Directorate-General V and to consider renaming the Directorate General as follows: 'Employment, Industrial Relations and Equal Opportunities'. There is an urgent need to develop policy in the area of equal opportunities for all citizens of the European Community, and in particular for disabled people

   (ii) to establish a new Directorate within DGV with the responsibility for developing policy initiatives in relation to equal opportunities legislation and to ensure that disabled people are employed at all levels within this new Directorate

   (iii) to publish in 1994 a Green Paper, the contents of which should include the UN Standard Rules on the Equalisation of Opportunities for disabled people, and an outline of the Commission's plans to initiate Community legislation for its adoption and implementation

   (iv) to present at the European Parliament of Disabled People, 3 December 1994, a report on the progress of the Green Paper on the UN Standard Rules on the Equalisation of Opportunities for disabled people, and the Commission's proposals for the introduction of Community legislation, including a comprehensive social policy initiative

3. Invites the Community institutions and the Member States of the European Community to support studies on human rights of disabled people, and to ensure that disabled people, through their representative organisations, are involved in all stages of the planning and management of such studies, and that the results of the studies are disseminated as widely as possible.

4. Invites the Community institutions and the Member States to adopt equal opportunities instruments in the areas of employment, contract compliance and funding criteria.

5. Invites the Community institutions and Member States to ensure that at the time of revision of the Treaty on European Union ('Maastricht'), a general anti-discrimination provision is included.

Article 17

1. No one shall be subjected to arbitrary or unlawful interference with his privacy, family, home or correspondence, nor to unlawful attacks on his honour and reputation.
2. Everyone has the right to the protection of the law against such interference or attacks.

Article 23

2. The right of men and women of marriageable age to marry and to found a family shall be recognised.

(I) International Day of Disabled People

Affirmation of commitment

We affirm that disabled people should share equally in all the rights, benefits, obligations and opportunities of their community, and should receive all support in reaching their full potential enjoying whatever improvement of living conditions and quality of life may result from social and economic development.

We believe it is an essential responsibility of governments and the community to promote effective measures for the prevention of disability, for the rehabilitation of those who are impaired and for the equalisation of opportunity for all.

We support continuing action to end discriminatory attitudes and practice in society and to provide a non-handicapping environment.

We affirm that disabled people, both as individuals and through their organisations, should be involved in the decision-making processes of policies and programmes that affect their lives.

We acknowledge that these principles apply with equal urgency in all communities. To ensure their effective application we urge all governments, in consultation with organisations of and working for disabled people, and using the World Programme of Action concerning Disabled Persons as a policy guideline, to formulate national, regional and local plans of action with achievable and sustainable targets to the year 2000 and beyond.

We support the United Nations in providing renewed leadership in moving towards a society for all in which disabled people can participate as equals.

Signed this third day of December, 1994

Source: Documents 4 and 5, Disability Awareness in Action: Consultation and Influence, Disability Awareness in Action (DAA), 11 Belgrave Road, London SW1V 1RB. (DAA is an international information project for disabled people and their organisations run by disabled people.)

Selected extracts from legislation and policy statements

(J) Selective abortion for unborn children with impairments

Selective abortion for unborn children with impairments was enshrined in law in 1967 with the introduction of the Abortion Act 1967.

Abortion Act 1967

'1. (1) Subject to the provisions of this section, a person shall not be guilty of an offence under the law relating to abortion when a pregnancy is terminated by a registered medical practitioner if two registered medical practitioners are of the opinion, formed in good faith –

  (a) that the continuance of the pregnancy would involve risk to the life of the pregnant woman, or of injury to the physical or mental health of the pregnant or any existing children of her family, greater than if the pregnancy were terminated; or

  (b) that there is a substantial risk that if the child were born it would suffer from such physical or mental abnormalities as to be seriously handicapped' (Abortion Act 1967).

(K) Meeting special educational needs

Section 10 of the Education Act 1976 was intended to replace Section 33 of the Education Act 1944. It would have given disabled children the right to attend mainstream schools. The date on which Section 10 would have come into force, however, was left to the discretion of the Secretary of State for Education. Provision had not been implemented when there was a change of government in 1979, and the incoming administration announced its intention of leaving Section 10 ineffective.

Education Act 1976 (Section 10)

'Pupils requiring special educational treatment.

  (10) (1) For Section 33(2) of the Education Act 1944 there shall be substituted –

    (2) The arrangements made by a local education authority for the special educational treatment of pupils of any such category shall, subject to subsection (2A) of this section, provide for the education of the pupils in county or voluntary schools.

(2A) Where the education of the pupils in such schools as aforesaid –

(a) is impracticable or incompatible with the provision of efficient instruction in the schools: or

(b) would involve unreasonable public expenditure, the arrangements may provide for the education of the pupils in special schools appropriate to the category to which the pupils belong or in schools not maintained by a local education authority and for the time being notified by the Secretary of State to the authority as in his opinion suitable for the purpose' (Education Act 1976).

In 1980 the Government produced 'Special Needs in Education' which oulined its proposals for implementing the recommendations of the 'Report of the Committee of Enquiry into the Education of Handicapped Children and Young People' chaired by Mary Warnock (HMSO 1978). Extracts from these proposals are reproduced below.

'Integration

35. There are legitimate differences of view over where and how a child with special educational needs is best educated. The Government takes as its starting point the principle that children and young people who have such needs should be educated in association with those who do not. But this principle must always be applied so as not to frustrate the aim of giving the child or student, within the limits of what is practicable, the greatest possible opportunity to benefit from the education process. The right placement for a child with a serious disability can only be properly determined after careful assessment of his needs by competent professionals and in close consultation with his parents. For some children with special needs association, or full association, with other children is the wrong solution and to impose it would be unfair to the child, his parents, other children and the taxpayer. In such a case the arguments for full association must give way to other arguments which are more valid in that case.

36. Accordingly the Government does not propose to bring into force Section 10 of the Education Act 1976. To do so would entail perpetuating the concept of categories of disability, because the section builds on the provision in the Education Act 1944 which incorporates that concept. But Section 10 is open to more general objections. It gives no opportunity to the expression of parental preference. It is too narrowly concerned with merely placing a handicapped pupil in an ordinary school, which does not by itself guarantee that the child will be educated in association with children who are not handicapped. Above all, it does not take sufficient account of the fact that every child has his own educational needs. Many handicapped children would stand less chance of having their needs met if they were obliged to attend the ordinary schools with their present facilities and resources. Yet in present economic circumstances there is no possibility of finding the massive additional resources for the education and health services which would be required to enable every ordinary school to provide an adequate education for children with serious educational difficulties, without thereby providing a less than adequate education for the other pupils.

37. The Government intends that the process of planned and sensible integration of handicapped children into ordinary schools should continue. However, children with serious difficulties must not be obliged to attend ordinary schools if these cannot fully provide for their needs. In the Government's

view, it will continue to be necessary to provide places in special schools and classes, and to make other special arrangements, e.g. through education at home or in hospital, for some of the most seriously handicapped children.

38. The development of the education service will need to take place within the financial limits set by the public expenditure plans which the Government has announced'.

The government's proposals

39. In accordance with the approach outlined in Section 11, the Government proposes legislation which will do away with the present system of special educational treatment for children ascertained as belonging to a category of handicap. Instead it proposes in this area to base the duties and powers of LEAs and schools, and the rights and duties of parents, on the concept that certain children have special educational needs. A minority of such children will, as the Warnock Committee recommended, be the subject of a formal record, on the basis of which the LEA, in the interest of the child, will take special steps in regard to his education and keep his progress under regular formal review . . .

Integration: statement of principle

41. The Government proposes that a child with special educational needs who is not a 'recorded' child should normally be educated in an ordinary school; and that a 'recorded' child shall also, wherever this is reasonable and practicable, be so educated. Accordingly the proposed legislation will provide that a child with special educational needs shall be educated with children without such needs, provided that the arrangements are capable of meeting his needs, are compatible with the efficient education of the children with whom he is to be educated, and with the efficient use of public resources, and take proper account of the wishes of his parents. This provision will replace Section 10 of the 1976 Education Act.

Special and independent schools

42. The adoption, on this basis, of the principle of integration makes it necessary to ensure that where a 'recorded' child cannot be educated at an ordinary school, alternative arrangements can be made available. The Government therefore proposes to retain the present system of maintained and non-maintained special schools whose arrangements are subject to the approval of the Secretary of State; and to augment it by a new category of independent schools which will be approved by the Secretary of State as suitable for the admission of 'recorded' children. As in the case of the special schools, approval will be conditional on the school's compliance with regulations governing its general conduct, staffing, premises and educational standards. The Secretary of State will maintain a list of all independent school suitable for the admission of 'recorded' children. An LEA will not normally be allowed to place a 'recorded' child in an independent school which is not on this list (Special Needs in Education 1980).

The Government's proposals became law with the introduction and implementation of the Education Act 1981. (Please note that this Act does not extend to Scotland or Northern Ireland.)

(L) The employment of disabled people

The employment quota scheme was introduced in the immediate post 1945 years with the Disabled Persons (Employment) Act 1944. Although never adequately supported by successive British governments and unable to deal with the problems of underemployment and discrimination in the workplace, we include the relevant extracts here because they represent the first and, hitherto, only serious attempt by a British government to secure the employment rights of disabled people through legislation.

Disabled Persons (Employment) Act 1944

'9. (1) It shall be the duty of a person who has a substantial number of employees to give employment to persons registered as handicapped by disablement to the number that is his quota as ascertained in accordance with the next succeeding section, and, where he is not already doing so at times when vacancies occur, to allocate vacancies for that purpose; and the said duty shall be enforceable to the extent and in manner hereinafter in this section applies, that is to say, a person who for the time being has, or in accordance with his normal practice and apart from transitory circumstances would have, in his employment persons to the number of not less than twenty (or such lower number as may be specified by an order made by the Minister for the time being in force).

Obligations as to employment of quota of registered persons in substantial staffs.

(2) Subject to the provisions of the two next succeeding subsections, a person to whom this subsection applies shall not at any time take, or offer to take, into his employment any person other than a person registered as handicapped by disablement, if immediately after the taking in of that person the number of persons so registered in the employment of the person to whom this section applies (excluding persons employed by him in an employment of a class then designated under Section 12 of this Act) would be less than his quota.

(3) Subsection (2) of this section shall not apply to a person's taking, or offering to take, into his employment at any time a person whom apart from that subsection it would have been his duty to take into his employment at that time either –
   (a) by virtue of any Act, whether passed before or after the passing of this Act; or
   (b) by virtue of an agreement to reinstate him in his employment entered into before the date appointed for the coming into operation of subsection (2) of this section.

(4) Subsection (2) of this section shall not apply to a person's taking, or offering to take, into his employment any person in accordance with a permit issued by the Minister under the subsequent provisions of this Act in that behalf.

(5) A person to whom this section applies who for the time being has in his employment a person registered as handicapped by disablement shall not, unless he has reasonable cause for doing so, discontinue the employment of that person, if immediately after the discontinuance the number of persons so registered in the employment of the person to whom this section applies (excluding persons employed by him in an employment of a class then' designated under section twelve of this Act) would be less than his quota:'

Provided that this subsection shall not have effect if immediately after the discontinuance the employer would no longer be a person to whom this section applies.

(6) Any person who contravenes subsection (2) or subsection (5) of this section shall be guilty of an offence and shall be liable on summary conviction to a fine not exceeding one hundred pounds or to imprisonment for a term not exceeding three months, or to both such fine and such imprisonment.

(7) A prosecution for a contravention of subsection (5) of this section shall not be instituted against any person unless –

(a) the matter has been referred to a district advisory committee;

(b) the committee, before considering the matter, has notified that person so as to give him an opportunity of making within a period not shorter than seven days from the sending or giving of the notification to him such representations to the committee as he may desire, either orally or in writing as he may desire; and

(c) the committee has made a report to the Minister. On any such prosecution it shall not be necessary to prove compliance with the preceding provisions of this subsection unless the defendant so requires, and, if he so requires, a certificate purporting to be signed by or on behalf of the chairman of a district advisory committee that the matter in question has been referred to the committee under this subsection and that a notification and report has been made by them as therein until the contrary is shown.'

The quota was set at three per cent, fines for non-compliance were never increased, and exemption permits were issued en masse. There were only ten prosecutions under the 1944 Act and one of these was dismissed. The last case was heard in 1975. There is substantial evidence too that disabled workers are paid less than non-disabled peers in mainstream employment and that discrimination both direct and indirect is widespread.

The quota scheme was abolished with the introduction of the 1995 Disability Discrimination Act (see below).

(M) Disability benefits

Prior to the introduction and general expansion of the disability benefits system in the 1970s, disabled people without work and not eligible for any type of war or industrial injury pension had to rely on means tested social security payments or charity. In 1971 a long term benefit to replace earnings known as 'Invalidity Benefit' was introduced for those who had worked but were no longer able due to acquired impairment resulting from chronic ill health or accident. Benefits to cover some of the additional costs of living with impairment in a non-disabled world soon followed. These included Attendance Allowance and Mobility Allowance.

Attendance Allowance

'15. (1) A person shall be entitled to an attendance allowance if he satisfies prescribed conditions as to residence or presence in Great Britain and either –
  (a) he is so severely disabled physically or mentally that, by day, he requires from another person either –
    (i) frequent attention throughout the day in connection with his bodily functions, or
    (ii) continual supervision throughout the day in order to avoid substantial danger to himself or others; or
  (b) he is so severely disabled physically or mentally that, at night, he requires from another person either –
    (i) prolonged or repeated attention during the night in connection with his bodily functions, or
    (ii) continual supervision throughout the night in order to avoid substantial danger to himself or others' (Social Security Act 1973).

Mobility Allowance

'37A. (1) Subject to the provisions of this section, a person who satisfies prescribed conditions as to residence or presence in Great Britain shall be entitled to a mobility allowance for any period throughout which he is suffering from physical disablement such that he is either unable to walk or virtually unable to do so.
  (2) Regulations may prescribe the circumstance in which a person is or is not to be treated for the purposes of this section as suffering from such physical disablement as is mentioned above; but a person qualifies for the allowance only if –
    (a) his inability or virtual inability to walk is likely to persist for at least 12 months from the time when a claim for the allowance is received by the Secretary of State; and
    (b) during most of that period his condition will be such as permits him from time to time to benefit from enhanced facilities for locomotion' (Social Security Act 1975).

In 1975 the 'Non-Contributory Invalidity Pension', later known as the Severe Disablement Allowance, was introduced for those people who had not paid sufficient National Insurance Contributions to receive Invalidity Benefit.

Non-Contributory Invalidity Pension

'6. (1) Subject to the provisions of this section, a person shall be entitled to a non-contributory invalidity pension for any day on which he is incapable of work if he has been incapable of work for a period of not less than one hundred and ninety-six consecutive days ending immediately before that day.

(2) A person shall not be entitled to any such pension if he is under the age of sixteen or receiving full-time education; and a woman shall not be entitled to any such pension if –
    (a) she is married and either –
        (i) she is residing with her husband; or
        (ii) he is contributing to her maintenance at a weekly rate not less than the weekly rate of such a pension; or
    (b) she is cohabitating with a man as his wife,

(3) A person shall not be entitled to any such pension unless he satisfies prescribed conditions as to residence or presence in Great Britain.

(4) A person who has attained pensionable age shall not be entitled to a pension under this section unless he was entitled (or is treated by regulations as having been entitled) to such a pension immediately before attaining that age; and regulations may make provision whereby a person who has attained retiring age and was entitled to such a pension immediately before attaining that age continues to be entitled to such a pension notwithstanding that he is not incapable of work or no longer satisfies the requirements of subsection (1) above as the period for which a person must have been incapable of work' (Social Security Pensions Act 1975).

Disability Living Allowance

Attendance Allowance and Mobility Allowance were effectively bundled together in 1991 as the Disability Living Allowance:

'378A (1) Disabled Living Allowance shall consist of a care component and a mobility component.
     (2) A person's entitlement to a Disability Living Allowance may be an entitlement to either component or to both of them' (Disability Living Allowance and Disability Working Allowance Act 1991).

Disability Working Allowance

Initially termed the 'Disability Employment Credit', the Disability Working Allowance was introduced in 1991. Available to people assessed by a doctor to be only partly capable of work and in receipt of disability or other benefits, it was designed to top up low earnings and so encourage people to accept or stay in low-paid employment.

'5.11 The Government believes the most important remaining gap in the existing structure of Social Security for disabled people is the absence of help targeted specifically on people who are only partially rather than wholly incapable of work. We propose to introduce a major new benefit to remedy this deficiency.

5.12 A Disability Employment Credit would encourage people to return to or take up work by topping up low earnings. The result would be improved incomes for at least some disabled people and improved opportunities for integration with non-disabled people. A Disability Employment Credit would also provide short-term rehabilitation help in the transition from unemployment to full-time work' (*The Way Ahead: Benefits for Disabled People*, 1990, 33–4).

However, because the Disability Working Allowance is means tested and because, like other social security payments, it has a tapered withdrawal as incomes rise, take up has been consistently poor.

Incapacity Benefit

In order to restrict access to the disability benefit system the government introduced yet more changes in 1994 with the 'Social Security (Incapacity for Work) Act 1994'.

'An Act to provide for incapacity benefit in place of sickness benefit and invalidity benefit: to make provision as to the test of incapacity for work for the purposes of that benefit and other social security purposes; to make provision as to the rate of statutory sick pay; to make other amendments as to certain allowances payable to a person who is or has been incapable of work; and for connected purposes' (Social Security (Incapacity for Work) Act 1994).

This Act imposed a stringent 'All Work' test on disabled claimants based on one-off functional tasks which excludes important factors such as age, training, job skills and accessibility. As a consequence people with invisible or fluctuating conditions such as arthritis, sickle cell anaemia, severe emotional distress or HIV/AIDS are particularly at risk of losing benefit. In many ways the Social Security (Incapacity for Work) Act signalled a hardening of government policy on disability benefits and indeed the benefit system as a whole.

(N) Community-based support services

The Chronically Sick and Disabled Persons Act 1970 was hailed by many as a 'charter for the disabled' (Topliss and Gould 1981). In conjunction with the Local Authority Social Services Act 1970 it signalled the setting up and expansion of local authority-run services for disabled people. In many respects, however, the Act, notably, Section 2, is little more than a re-emphasis of Section 29 of the National Assistance Act 1948. Also, it is important to note that implementation for much of the Act was not compulsory, nor was it free. Included below are extracts illustrating the extensive nature of the Act; namely, General Note, and Sections 1–8.

Chronically Sick and Disabled Persons Act 1970

'General Note

This Act makes further provision with respect to the welfare of chronically sick and disabled persons.

S. 1 imposes on local authorities a duty to inform themselves as to the need for and existence of welfare services. S. 2 concerns the provision of welfare services and S. 3 the duties of housing authorities. S. 4 deals with access to, and facilities at, premises open to the public. S. 5 relates to the provision of public sanitary conveniences. S. 6 concerns the provision of sanitary conveniences at certain premises open to the public. S. 7 provides for signs at buildings complying with SS. 4–6. S. 8 deals with access to, and facilities at, university and school buildings. S. 9 concerns the central advisory committee on war pensions, S. 10 Housing Advisory Committees, S. 11 the National Insurance Advisory Committee, S. 12 the Industrial Injuries Advisory Council, S. 13 the Youth Employment Service and S. 14 miscellaneous advisory committees. S. 15 provides for the co-option of chronically sick or disabled persons to local authority committees and S. 16 specifies the duties of the national advisory council established under S. 17 of the Disabled Persons (Employment) Act 1944. S. 17 provides for the separation of younger from older hospital patients, S. 18 concerns information as to accommodation of younger with older persons under Part III of the National Assistance Act 1948 and S. 19 deals with the provision of information relating to chiropody services. S. 20 concerns the use of invalid carriages on highways and S. 21 provides that badges shall be issued for display on motor vehicles used by disabled persons. S. 22 relates to an annual report on research and development work. S. 23 concerns war pensions appeals. S. 24 deals with the institute of hearing research. S. 25 makes provision for special educational treatment for the deaf-blind and S. 26 for children suffering from acute dyslexia. S. 28 empowers the Secretary of State to make regulations defining certain expressions and S. 29 contains short title, extent and commencement.

The Act, which does not apply to Northern Ireland, except as expressly provided by SS. 9, 14, 23, applies to Scotland with the exception of SS. 1–2. The Act received the Royal Assent on May 29, 1970, and comes into force as follows: SS. 1, 21 on a date to be appointed, SS. 4–8 on November 29, 1970 and the remainder on August 29, 1970'.

'Scotland

The Act (except SS. 1, 2) does not apply to Scotland (S. 26(2)).

Welfare and Housing

Information as to need for and existence of welfare services

1. (1) It shall be the duty of every local authority having functions under section 29 of the National Assistance Act 1948 to inform themselves of the number of persons to whom that section applies within their area and of the need for the making by the authority of arrangements under that section for such persons.
   (2) Every such local authority –
       (a) shall cause to be published from time to time as such times and in such manner as they consider appropriate general information as to the services provided under arrangements made by the authority under the said section 29 which are for the time being available in their area; and

(b) shall ensure that any such person as aforesaid who uses any of those services is informed of any other of those services which in the opinion of the authority is relevant to his needs.

(3) This section shall come into operation on such date as the Secretary of State may by order made by statutory instrument appoint.

Provision of welfare services

2. (1) Where a local authority having functions under section 29 of the National Assistance Act 1948 are satisfied in the case of any person to whom that section applies who is ordinarily resident in their area that it is necessary in order to meet the needs of that person for that authority to make arrangements for all or any of the following matters, namely –

(a) the provision of practical assistance for that person in his home;

(b) the provision for that person of, or assistance to that person in obtaining, wireless, television, library or similar recreational facilities;

(c) the provision for that person of lectures, games, outings or other recreational facilities outside his home or assistance to that person in taking advantage of educational facilities available to him;

(d) the provision for that person of facilities for, or assistance in, travelling to and from his home for the purpose of participating in any services provided under arrangements made by the authority under the said section 29 or, with the approval of the authority, in any services provided otherwise than as aforesaid which are similar to services which could be provided under such arrangements;

(e) the provision of assistance for that person in arranging for the carrying out of any works of adaptation in his home or the provision of any additional facilities designed to secure his greater safety, comfort or convenience;

(f) facilitating the taking of holidays by that person, whether at holiday homes or otherwise and whether provided under arrangements made by the authority or otherwise;

(g) the provision of meals for that person whether in his home or elsewhere;

(h) the provision for that person of, or assistance to that person in obtaining, a telephone and any special equipment necessary to enable him to use a telephone,

Then, notwithstanding anything in any scheme made by the authority under the said section 29, but subject to the provisions of section 35(2) of that Act (which requires local authorities to exercise their functions under Part III of that Act under the general guidance of the Secretary of State and in accordance with the provisions of any regulations made for the purpose), it shall be the duty of that authority to make those arrangements in exercise of their functions under the said section 29.

(2) Without prejudice to the said section 35(2), subsection (3) of the said section 29 (which requires any arrangements made by a local authority under that section to be carried into effect in accordance with a scheme made thereunder) shall not apply –

(a) to any arrangements made in pursuance of subsection (1) of this section; or

(b) in the case of a local authority who have made such a scheme, to any arrangements made by virtue of subsection (1) of the said section 29 in addition to those required or authorised by the scheme which are so made with the approval of the Secretary of State.

Duties of housing authorities

3. (1) Every local authority for the purposes of Part V of the Housing Act 1957 in discharging their duty under section 91 of that Act to consider housing conditions in their district and the needs of the district with respect to the provision of further housing accommodation shall have regard to the special needs of chronically sick or disabled persons; and any proposals prepared and submitted to the Minister by the authority under that section for the provision of new houses shall distinguish any houses which the authority propose to provide which make special provision for the needs of such persons.

   (2) In the application of this section to Scotland for the words 'Part V of the Housing Act 1957', '91' and 'Minister' there shall be substituted respectively the words 'Part VII of the Housing (Scotland) Act 1966', '137' and 'Secretary of State.'

Premises open to public

Access to, and facilities at, premises open to the public

4. (1) Any person undertaking the provision of any building or premises to which the public are to be admitted, whether on payment or otherwise, shall, in the means of access both to and within the building or premises, and in the parking facilities and sanitary conveniences to be available (if any), make provision, in so far as it is in the circumstances both practicable and reasonable, for the needs of members of the public visiting the building or premises who are disabled.

   (2) This section shall not apply to any building or premises intended for purposes mentioned in subsection (2) of section 8 of this Act.

Provision of public sanitary conveniences

5. (1) Where any local authority undertakes the provision of a public sanitary convenience, it shall be the duty of the authority, in doing so, to make provision, in so far as it is in the circumstances both practicable and reasonable, for the needs of disabled persons.

   (2) Any local authority which in any public sanitary convenience provided by them make or have made provision for the needs of disabled persons shall take such steps as may be reasonable, by sign-posts or similar notices, to indicate the whereabouts of the convenience.

   (3) In this section 'local authority' means a local authority within the meaning of the Local Government Act 1933 or the Local Government (Scotland) Act 1947 and any joint board or joint committee of which all the constituent authorities are local authorities within the meaning of either of those Acts.

*Provision of sanitary conveniences at certain premises open
to the public*

6. (1) Any person upon whom a notice is served with respect to any premises
    under section 89 of the Public Health Act 1936 (which empowers local
    authorities by notice to make requirements as to the provision and main-
    tenance of sanitary conveniences for the use of persons frequenting
    certain premises used for the accommodation, refreshment or entering
    certain premises used for the accommodation, refreshment or entertain-
    ment of members of the public) shall in complying with that notice
    make provision, in so far as it is in the circumstances both practicable
    and reasonable, for the needs of persons frequenting those premises who
    are disabled.
   (2) The owner of a building, who has been ordered under section 11(4) of
    the Building (Scotland) Act 1959 to make the building conform to a
    provision of building standards regulations make under section 3 of that
    Act requiring the provision of suitable and sufficient sanitary conveni-
    ences therein, shall in complying with that order make provision, in so
    far as it is in the circumstances both practicable and reasonable, for the
    needs of persons frequenting that building who are disabled.

Signs at buildings complying with SS. 4–6

7. (1) Where any provision required by or under section 4, 5 or 6 of this Act is
    made at a building in compliance with that section, a notice or sign
    indicating that provision is made for the disabled shall be displayed
    outside the building or so as to be visible from outside it.
   (2) This section applies to a sanitary convenience provided elsewhere than
    in a building, and not itself being a building, as it applies to a building.

University and school buildings

Access to, and facilities at, university and school buildings

8. (1) Any person undertaking the provision of a building intended for pur-
    poses mentioned in subsection (2) below shall, in the means of access
    both to and within the building, and in the parking facilities and sanitary
    conveniences to be available (if any), make provision, in so far as it is
    in the circumstances both practicable and reasonable, for the needs of
    persons using the buildings who are disabled.
   (2) The purposes referred to in subsection (1) above are the purposes of any
    of the following:
     (a) universities, university colleges and colleges, schools and halls of
        universities;
     (b) schools within the meaning of the Education Act 1944, teacher train-
        ing colleges maintained by local education authorities in England or
        Wales and other institutions providing further education pursuant to
        a scheme under section 42 of that Act;
     (c) educational establishments within the meaning of the Education
        (Scotland) Act 1962' (Chronically Sick and Disabled Persons Act
        1970).

Despite the above, provision remained essentially *ad hoc* and character-ised by substantial parochial variation. In response, the government intro-duced the Disabled Persons (Services Consultation and Representation) Act 1986.

Disabled Persons (Services Consultation and Representation) Act 1986

'An Act to provide for the improvement of the effectiveness of, and the co-ordination of resources in, the provision of services for people with mental or physical handicap and for people with mental illness; to make further provision for the assessment of the needs of such people; to establish further consultative processes and representational rights for such people; and for connected pur-poses'. (Disabled Persons (Services Consultation and Representation) Act 1986)

In 1991 key sections of the 1986 Act which were intended to secure the right of disabled people to have an advocate had they needed one, and given them the right to ask local authorities for services, and to have a written statement on their needs assessment were officially scrapped. Furthermore, Section 10 of the Act specified quite clearly that repres-entatives of organisations of disabled people should be co-opted and involved in the planning and delivery of services. Research from both official and independent sources shows that this did not occur (Bewley and Glendinning 1992; Warburton 1990; Morris 1993).

A report published in 1988 by Sir Roy Griffith, then Vice Chair of the National Health Service management board, called for an end to the 'fragmentation and confusion' that characterised community-based support services. His recommendations were incorporated into the Gov-ernment White Paper *Caring for People* (1989) and the *National Health Service and Community Care Act* (1990). The thrust of the proposals are summarised below.

Caring for People (1989) and the National Health Service and Community Care Act 1990

'The Government's Approach to Achieving Better Care

1.8 The Government believes that for most people community care offers the best form of care available – certainly with better quality and choice than they might have expected in the past. The changes outlined in this White Paper are intended to:
   • enable people to live as normal a life as possible in their own homes or in a homely environment in the local community;
   • provide the right amount of care and support to help people achieve maximum independence and by acquiring or reacquiring basic living skills, help them to achieve their full potential;
   • give people a greater individual say in how they live their lives and the services they need to do so.

Promoting choice and independence underlines all the Government's proposals.

1.9 The Government acknowledges that the great bulk of community care is provided by friends, family and neighbours. The decision to take on a caring role is never an easy one. However many people make that choice and it is right that they should be able to play their part looking after those that are close to them. But it must be recognised that carers need help and support if they are to continue to carry out their role; and many people will not have carers readily available who can meet all their needs.

1.10 The Government therefore believes that the key components of community care should be:
   • services that respond flexibly and sensitively to the needs of individuals and their carers;
   • services that allow a range of options for consumers;
   • services that intervene no more than is necessary to foster independence;
   • services that concentrate on those with the greatest needs.

Key objectives

1.11 The Government's proposals have six key objectives for service delivery:
   • *to promote the development of domiciliary day and respite services to enable people to live in their own homes wherever feasible and sensible.* Existing funding structures have worked against the development of such services. In future the Government will encourage the targeting of home-based services on those people whose need for them is greatest.
   • *to ensure that service providers make practical support for carers a high priority.* Assessment of care needs should always take account of the needs of caring family and friends.
   • *to make proper assessment of need and good case management the cornerstone of high quality care.* Packages of care should then be designed with individual needs and preferences.
   • *to promote the development of a flourishing independent sector alongside good quality public services.* The Government has endorsed Sir Roy Griffith's recommendations that social service authorities should be 'enabling' agencies. It will be their responsibility to make maximum possible use of private and voluntary providers, and so increase the available range of options and widen consumer choice.
   • *to clarify the responsibilities of agencies and so make it easier to hold them to account for their performance.* The Government recognises that the present confusion has contributed to poor overall performance.
   • *to secure better value for taxpayers' money by introducing a new funding structure for social care.* The Government's aim is that security provisions should not, as they do now, provide any incentives in favour of residential and nursing home care.

Key Changes

1.12 In order to achieve these objectives, the Government proposes to make a number of changes in the way in which the social care is delivered and funded:

First, local authorities are to become responsible, in collaboration with medical, nursing and other interests, for assessing individual need, designing care arrangements and securing their delivery within available resources:

second, local authorities will be expected to produce and publish clear plans for the development of community care services, consistent with the plans of health authorities and other interested agencies. The Government will take new powers to ensure that plans are open to inspection, and to call for reports from social service authorities:

third, local authorities will be expected to make maximum use of the independent sector. The government will ensure that they have acceptable plans for achieving this:

fourth, there will be a new funding structure for those seeking public support for residential and nursing home care from April 1991. After that date local authorities will take responsibility for financial support of people in private and voluntary homes over and above any general social security entitlements. The new arrangements will not, however, apply to people already resident in homes before April 1991.

fifth, applicants with few or no resources of their own will be eligible for the same levels of Income Support and Housing Benefit, irrespective of whether they are living in their own homes or in independent residential or nursing homes:

sixth, local authorities will be required to establish inspection and registration units at arms length from the management of their own services which will be responsible for checking on standards in both their own homes and in independent sector residential care homes:

seventh, there will be a new specific grant to promote the development of social care for seriously mentally ill people'.

(Caring for People 1989: 4–6)

After long and consistent lobbying by disabled people and their organisations the government introduced the Community Care (Direct Payments) Act in 1996. This enables local authorities to make payments directly to disabled individuals to employ their own personal assistant/s. Hitherto, such payments had been illegal under Section 29 of the 1948 National Assistance Act and Section 45 of the 1986 Disabled Persons (Services Consultation and Representation) Act.

Community Care (Direct Payments) Act 1996

'An Act to enable local authorities responsible for community care services to make payments to persons in respect of their securing the provision of such services; and for connected purposes.

England and Wales

1. (1) Where –

> (a) an authority have decided under section 47 of the National Health Service and Community Care Act 1990 (assessment by local authorities

of needs for community care services) that the needs of a person call for the provision of any community care services, and

(b) the person is of a description which is specified for the purposes of this subsection by regulations made by the Secretary of State, the authority may, if the person consents, pay to him the whole, or such part as they think fit, of the cost of his securing the provision of any of the services for which they have decided his needs call.

(2) If –

(a) an authority pay under subsection (1) above at a rate below their estimate of the reasonable cost of securing the provision of the service concerned, and

(b) the payee satisfies the authority that his means are insufficient and for it to be reasonably practical for him to make up the difference, the authority shall so adjust the payment to him under the subsection as to avoid there being a greater difference than that which appears to them to be reasonably practicable for him to make up.

(3) In the case of a service which, apart from this Act, would be provided under section 117 of the Mental Health Act 1983 (After Care), an authority shall not pay under subsection (1) above at a rate below their estimate of the reasonable cost of securing the provision of the service' (Community Care (Direct Payments) Act 1996).

It is important to remember here that this Act is not mandatory it is permissive. Hence, local authorities can choose not to make direct payments if they so wish. Disabled people therefore do not have a right to direct payments in lieu of services. Moreover, even where direct payments are paid disabled people under eighteen and over retirement age are excluded.

(O) Combating discrimination against disabled people

The Disability Discrimination Act 1995 is an important piece of legislation as it signifies official recognition that discrimination against disabled people is a major problem. As we have shown in Part One, the Act represents a governmental response to a campaign for equal treatment for disabled people which spans over three decades. The first attempt to introduce civil rights legislation for disabled people was made by Lord Ashley in 1982; there have been fourteen unsuccessful attempts since. Included below is the general statement of the Act and an extract from Part One which deals with the definition of disability.

Disability Discrimination Act 1995

'An Act to make it unlawful to discriminate against disabled persons in connection with employment, the provision of goods, facilities and services or the disposal or management of premises; to make provision about the employment of disabled persons; and to establish a National Disability Council. (8 November 1995)

BE IT ENACTED by the Queen's most Excellent Majesty, by and with the advice and consent of the Lords Spiritual and Temporal, and Commons, in this present Parliament assembled, and by the authority of the same, as follows:

Part 1

Disability

1. (1) Subject to the provisions of Schedule 1, a person has a disability for the purposes of this Act if he has a physical or mental impairment which has a substantial and long-term adverse effect on his ability to carry out normal day-to-day activities. Meaning of 'disability' and 'disabled person'.
   (2) In this Act 'disabled person' means a person who has a disability.

Given the gross inadequacies of this particular piece of legislation it is highly unlikely that it will survive into the twenty-first century in its present form.

Table of selected relevant statutes and regulations

1893 Elementary Education (Blind and Deaf Children) Act
1899 Elementary Education (Defective and Epileptic Children) Act
1911 National Insurance Act
1918 Education Act
1919 Disabled Men (Facilities for Employment) Act
1920 Blind Persons Act
1944 Disabled Persons (Employment) Act
1944 Education Act
1946 National Health Service Act
1948 National Assistance Act
1958 Disabled Persons (Employment) Act
1967 Abortion Act
1969 Mental Health Act
1970 National Insurance (Old Persons' and Widows' Pensions and Attendance Allowance) Act
1970 Chronically Sick and Disabled Persons Act
1970 Education (Handicapped Children) Act
1971 National Insurance Act
1973 Social Security Act
1975 Social Security Pensions Act
1975 Social Security Benefits Act
1976 Education Act
1978 Rating (Disabled Persons) Act
1980 Housing Act
1980 Social Security Act
1980 Social Security (No. 2) Act
1981 The Education Act
1986 Disabled Persons (Services Consultation and Representation) Act
1987 Income support (General Regulations)
1988 Disability Grants
1988 Social Fund (General Regulations)
1988 Education Reform Act
1989 Children Act
1990 Human Fertilisation and Embryology Act
1990 National Health Service and Community Care Act
1991 Disability Living Allowance and Disability Working Allowance Act
1994 Social Security (Incapacity for Work) Act
1995 Disability Discrimination Act
1996 Community Care (Direct Payments) Act

Table of selected relevant official reports

1943 *Report of the Inter-Departmental Committee on the Rehabilitation and Resettlement of Disabled Persons*, HMSO

1957 *Report of the Committee of Inquiry on the Rehabilitation, Training and Resettlement of Disabled Persons*, HMSO

1957 *Royal Commission on the Law Relating to Mental Illness and Mental Deficiency*, HMSO

1968 *Report of the Committee on Local Authority and Allied Personal Social Services*, HMSO

1971 Department of Employment, *Services for the Disabled*, HMSO

1971 Office of Population Censuses and Surveys, *Handicapped and Impaired in Great Britain*, HMSO

1972 *Report of a Sub-Committee of the Standing Medical Advisory Committee, Rehabilitation*, HMSO

1972 *Report of the Committee of Enquiry into the Education of the Visually Handicapped*, HMSO

1972 Department of Employment discussion document, *Resettlement Policy and Services for Disabled People*, HMSO

1973 Department of Employment discussion document, *Quota Scheme for Disabled People*, HMSO

1973 Department of Employment discussion document, *Sheltered Employment for Disabled People*, HMSO

1974 Department of Health and Social Security, *Mobility of Physically Disabled People*, HMSO

1975 Department of Health and Social Security, *Better Services for the Mentally Ill*, HMSO

1976 Department of Health and Social Security, *Priorities for Health and Personal Social Services*, HMSO

1976 *Report of the Committee on Child Health Services*, HMSO

1976 Department of Health and Social Security, *Report of the Working Party on Manpower Training for the Social Services*, HMSO

1976 Department of Health and Social Security, *Review of the Mental Health Act 1959*, HMSO

1978 *Report of the Royal Commission on Civil Liability and Compensation for Personal Injury*, HMSO

1978 *Special Educational Needs: Report of the Committee of Enquiry into the Education of Children and Young People*, HMSO

1979 *Report of the Committee of Enquiry into Mental Handicap Nursing and Care*, HMSO

1979 Manpower Services Commission discussion document, *Sheltered Employment for Disabled People*, HMSO

1980 Department of Education and Science, *Special Needs in Education*, HMSO

1980 Department of Health and Social Services, *Report on Inequalities in Health*, HMSO

1982 CORAD, *Report by the Committee on Restrictions Against Disabled People*, HMSO

1982 Department of the Environment, *Organizing House Adaptations for Disabled People*, HMSO

1986 Audit Commission, *Making a Reality of Community Care*, HMSO

1986 Department of Education and Science, *Report by HMI Inspectors on A Survey of Science in Special Education*, HMSO

1986 Department of Health and Social Security, *Review of Artificial Limb and Appliance Centre Services (Volumes 1 and 2)*, HMSO

1987 Department of Health and Social Security, *From Home Help to Home Care: an Analysis of Policy, Resourcing and Service Management*, HMSO

1988 Department of Employment, Employment *Services, Code of Good Practice on the Employment of Disabled People*: 2nd edn, HMSO

1988 Department of Health and Social Security, *Residential Care for Younger Physically Disabled Adults: The Research Reviewed*, HMSO

1988 Department of Health and Social Security, *The Griffiths Report: Community Care: Agenda for Action*, HMSO

1988 Office of Populations, Censuses and Surveys, *The Prevalence of Disability Among Adults*, HMSO

1988 Office of Populations, Censuses and Surveys, *The Financial Circumstances of Disabled Adults*, HMSO

1989 Department of Education and Science, *Report by HMI Inspectors on Educating Physically Disabled Pupils*, HMSO

1989 Department of Education and Science, *Report by HMI Inspectors on the Effectiveness of Small Special Schools*, HMSO

1989 Department of Education and Science, *A Survey of Support Services for SEN*, HMSO

1989 Department of Employment, *Employment Services: The Net Exchequer Costs of Sheltered Employment*, HMSO

1989 Department of Employment, *Employment Services, Evaluation of the Services Provided for People with Disabilities Outside the Disablement Resettlement Services*, HMSO

1989 Department of Health of Social Security, *Caring For People: Community Care in the Next Decade and Beyond*, HMSO

1989 Office of Populations, Censuses and Surveys, *Disabled Adults: Services, Transport and Employment*, HMSO

1989 Office of Populations, Censuses and Surveys, *The Prevalence of Disability Among Children*, HMSO

1989   Office of Populations, Censuses and Surveys, *Disabled Children: Services, Transport and Education*, HMSO

1989   Office of Populations, Censuses and Surveys, *The Financial Circumstances of Families with Disabled Children Living in Private Households*, HMSO

1990   Department of Employment, *Employment Services, Employment and Training for People with Disabilities: Consultative Document*, HMSO

1990   Department of Employment, *Employment Services: Self Identification of People with Disabilities Questions: Pilot*, HMSO

1990   Department of Employment, *Employment Services, Evaluation of Jobclub Provision for People with Disabilities*, HMSO

1990   Department of Employment, *Employment Services, A Report on the Organization of Special Jobcentre Services for People with Disabilities*, HMSO

1990   Department of Employment, *Employment Services, The Employment of People with Disabilities: Research into the Policies and Practices of Employers*, HMSO

1990   Department of the Environment, *The Building Regulations 1985 – Part M: Access for Disabled People*, HMSO

1990   Department of Health, *Community Care in the Next Decade and Beyond: Policy Guidance*, HMSO

1990   Department of Health, *Social Services Inspectorate, Developing Services for Disabled People*, HMSO

1990   Department of Social Security, *Disability Allowance: Assessment and Adjudication*, HMSO

1990   Department of Social Security, *The Way Ahead: Benefits for Disabled People*, HMSO

1990   Department of Transport, *Draft Directive on Mobility Improvement Measures for Workers with Reduced Mobility*, HMSO

1990   House of Commons Commission on Citizenship, *Encouraging Citizenship: Report of the House of Commons Commission on Citizenship*, HMSO

1990   House of Commons Social Security Committee, *Community Care: Social Security for Disabled People* (9th Report), HMSO

1991   Department of Health: *Social Services Inspectorate, Care Management and Assessment: Summary of Practice Guidance*, HMSO

1991   Department of the Environment, *Access Officers – National Survey: Summary of Designated Officers*, HMSO

1992   Audit Commission, *Getting in on the Act: Provision for Pupils with Special Educational Needs, The National Picture*, HMSO

1992   Department of Health, *The Costs of Informal Caring*, HMSO

1993   Department of Employment, *Employment Services, Employment Policies for Disabled People: A Review of Legislation and Services in Fifteen Different Countries*, HMSO

1993   Department of Health, *Community Care in a Multi-Racial Britain*, HMSO

1995   Social Services Inspectorate, *Growing Up and Moving On: Report on SSI Project on Transitional Services for Disabled Young People*, HMSO

1997   Department for Education and Employment, *Excellence for All Children: Meeting Special Educational Needs*, London

Table of selected relevant non-official reports

1964   United Nations Department of Social Economic Affairs, *Study on the Legislative and Administrative Aspects of Rehabilitation of the Disabled in Selected Countries*

1973   Economist Intelligence Unit report, *Care with Dignity*, National Fund for Research into Crippling Diseases, Sussex

1974   Disablement Income Group, *Realising a National Disability Income*, London

1976   Snowdon Working Party Report, *Integrating the Disabled*, National Fund for Research into Crippling Diseases, Sussex

1977   Personal Social Services Council, *Residential Care Reviewed*, London

1978   Economist Intelligence Unit *Whose Benefit?*, London

1979   Silver Jubilee *Committee Report on Improving Access for Disabled People, Can Disabled People Go Where You Go?*, DHSS

1985   Carnegie United Kingdom Trust, *Arts and Disabled People: The Attenborough Report*, London

1985   Inner London Education Authority, *Educational Opportunities for All*, London

1986   British Council of Organizations of Disabled People Report, *Disabled Young People Living Independently*, London

1986   Greater London Association for Disabled People, *All Change: A Consumer Study of Transport Handicap in Greater London*, London

1986   Royal College of Physicians of London, *Physical Disability in 1986 and Beyond*, London

1986   The Spastics Society, *An Equal Chance for Disabled People: A Study of Discrimination in Employment*, London

1987   British Council of Organizations of Disabled People Report, *Disabled People Looking at Housing*, London

1987   Disability Alliance, *Poverty and Disability, Breaking the Link: The Case for a Comprehensive Disability Income*, London

1987   SKILL: National Bureau for Handicapped Students, *Catching Up: A Survey of Provision for Students with Special Educational Needs in Further and Higher Education*, London

1987   The Spastics Society, *Disabled People and the 1987 General Election*, London

1988   Carnegie Council Review, *After Attenborough: Arts and Disabled People*, London

1988 Disabled Persons Transport Advisory Committee, *Public Transport and the Missing Six Millions: What Can be Learned?*, London

1988 Kings Fund Institute, *Last on the List: London*

1988 Prince of Wales Advisory Group on Disability, *Living Options Lottery*, London

1989 Disablement Income Group, *Not the OPCS Survey: Being Disabled Costs More Than They Said*, London

1990 Disablement Income Group, *Short Changed by Disability*, London

1990 Helen Hamlyn Foundation, *Lifetime Homes: Flexible Housing for Successive Generations*, London

1990 National Association of Citizens Advice Bureaux, *Assessing the Assessors: Medical Assessments for Disability Benefits*, London

1990 Social and Community Planning Research, *Employment and Handicap*, London

1990 Shelter, *Freedom to Lose: Housing Policy and People with Disabilities*, London

1990 Shelter, *Our Homes, Our Rights: Housing, Independent Living and Physically Disabled People*, London

1990 The Spastics Society, *An Equal Chance or No Chance?* London

1991 British Council of Organisations of Disabled People, *Disabled People in Britain and Discrimination: The Case for Anti-Discrimination Legislation*, Belper

1991 Policy Studies Institute, *Disability and Social Policy*, London

1992 The British Council of Organisations of Disabled People, *Disabling Imagery: An Exploration of Media Portrayals of Disabled People*, Derby

1992 Shelter, *Building our Lives: Housing, Independent Living and Disabled People*, London

1993 British Council of Organisations of Disabled People, *Making Our Own Choices: Independent Living, Personal Assistance and Disabled People*, Derby

1993 Excel Employment, *Barriers to Employment of Disabled People*, London

1993 Independent Living Fund, *Taking Care in the Market*, London

1993 Independent Living Fund, *Making Community Care a Reality*, London

1993 Joseph Rowntree Foundation, *Community Care or Independent Living*, York

1993 National Institute for Social Work, *Practical Experiences of Building a Challenge to Change: User Led Services*, London

1993 National Institute for Social Work, *The Shape of Things to Come? User Led Services*, London

1993 Social Policy Research Unit, *Moving in Old Age: New Directions in Housing Policy*, London

1993 Manpower Studies Institute, *Employers' Attitudes Towards People with Disabilities*, London

1993 Policy Studies Institute, *The Economic Problems of Disabled People*, London

1994   Policy Studies Institute, *Caring About Independence: Disabled People and The Independent Living Fund*, London

1994   Policy Studies Institute, *Employment Rehabilitation for Disabled People*, London

1994   Scope, *Wheel Power? Case Studies of Users and Providers of NHS Wheelchair Services*, London

1994   Social Policy Research Unit, *Unequal Opportunities: Growing Up Disabled*, London

1995   British Council of Organisations of Disabled People, *Demolishing Special Needs: Fundamental Principles of Non-discriminatory Housing*, Derby

1995   British Council of Organisations of Disabled People, *From National to Local: An Evaluation of the Effectiveness of National Disablement Information Providers' Services to Local Disablement Information Providers*, York

1995   Disability Alliance and the Disability Incomes Group, *There May be Trouble Ahead*, London

1995   Joseph Rowntree Foundation, *Service User Involvement: Synthesis of Findings and Experience in the Field of Community Care*, London

1995   Policy Studies Institute, *Access to Information: A Survey of the Provision of Disability Information*, London

1995   Scope, *Disabled in Britain: Counting on Community Care*, London

1995   Sheffield Citizens Advice Bureaux, *Debt Support Unit, Disability and Debt: The Experience of Disabled People in Debt*, Sheffield

1996   Disablement Income Group, *Personal Assistant Support Schemes and the Introduction of Direct Payments – A Report and Recommendations*, London

1996   Disablement Income Group, *Facilitating and Supporting Independent Living*, London

1996   Institute of Employment Studies, *The Recruitment and Retention of People with Disabilities*, London

1996   Joseph Rowntree Foundation, *Independent Living: A Review*, York

1996   Northern Officers Group, *The Disability Discrimination Act: A Policy and Practice Guide for Local Government and Disabled People*, London

1996   Social and Community Planning Research, *The Access to Work Programme – A Survey of Recipients, Employers, Employment Service Managers*, London

1996   Social and Community Planning Research and the Disability Alliance, *The Cost of Care: The Impact of Changing Policy on the Lives of Disabled People*, London

1996   Social Policy Research Unit, *Social Security and Mental Health: The Impact of Disabled Living Allowance*, York

REFERENCES

Abberley, P. (1987) 'The concept of oppression and the development of a social theory of disability', *Disability, Handicap and Society*, **2** (1), 5–19.

Abberley, P. (1991) 'The significance of the OPCS disability surveys', in Oliver, M. (ed.) *Social Work; Disabled People and Disabling Environments*, Jessica Kingsley Publishers, London.

Abberley, P. (1996) 'Disabled by numbers', in Levitas, R. and Guy, W. (eds) *Interpreting Official Statistics*, Routledge, London.

Ackernecht, E. H. (1971) *Medicine and Ethnology*, Johns Hopkins University, Baltimore.

Albrecht, G. (1992) *The Disability Business*, Sage, London.

Anderson, E. M., Clarke, L. and Swain, B. (1982) *Disability in Adolescence*, Methuen, London.

Ang, I. (1996) *Living Room Wars*, Routledge, London.

Anspach, R. (1979) 'From stigma to identity politics', *Social Science and Medicine*, **134**, 765–73.

Audit Commission (1986) *Making a Reality of Community Care*, HMSO, London.

Audit Commission (1992) *Getting in on the Act: Provision for Pupils with Special Educational Needs: The National Picture*, HMSO, London.

Barnes, C. (1990) *Cabbage Syndrome: The Social Construction of Dependency*, Falmer Press, London.

Barnes, C. (1991) *Disabled People in Britain and Discrimination: A Case for Anti-Discrimination Legislation*, Hurst, London.

Barnes, C. (1992) *Disabling Imagery: An Exploration of Media Portrayals of Disabled People*, The British Council of Organisations of Disabled People, Derby.

Barnes, C. (ed.) (1993) *Making our own Choices: Independent Living, Personal Assistance and Disabled People*, British Council of Organizations of Disabled People, Derby.

Barnes, C. (1995) *From National to Local: An Evaluation of National Disability Information Providers' Services to Local Disability Information Providers*, British Council of Organisations of Disabled People, Derby.

Barnes, C. and Oliver, M. (1995) 'Disability rights: rhetoric and reality in the UK', *Disability and Society*, **10** (4), 111–16.

Barton, R. W. (1959) *Institutional Neurosis*, John Wright, Bristol.

BCODP (1997) Personal communication, Litchuch Plaza, Derby, 24 September.

Beardshaw, V. (1988) *Last on the List: Community Services for People with Physical Disabilities*, King's Fund Institute, London.

Beazley, S. and Moore, M. (1995) *Deaf Children, Their Families and Professionals*, David Fulton, London.

Beresford, P. and Wallcraft, J. (1997) 'Psychiatric system survivors and emancipatory research: issues, overlaps and differences', in Barnes, C. and Mercer, G. (eds) *Doing Disability Research*, The Disability Press, Leeds.

Berthoud, R., Lakey, J. and McKay, S. (1993) *The Economic Problems of Disabled People*, Policy Studies Institute, London.

Bewley, C. and Glendinning, C. (1992) *Involving Disabled People in Community Care Planning*, Joseph Rowntree Foundation, York.

Biklen, D. and Bogdana, R. (1977) 'Media portrayals of disabled people: a study of stereotypes', *Inter Racial Children's Book Bulletin*, nos 8, 6 and 7.

Blaxter, M. (1980) *The Meaning of Disability*, 2nd edn, Heinemann, London.

Bogdan, R. (1988) *Freak Show: Presenting Human Oddities for Amusement and Profit*, Chicago University Press, Chicago.

Borsay, A. (1986) *Disabled People in the Community*, Bedford Square Press, London.

Bracking, S. (1993) 'An introduction to the idea of independent/integrated living' in *Making Our Own Choices; Independent Living, Personal Assistance and Disabled People*, pp. 12–14, The British Council of Organisations of Disabled People, Derby.

Brisenden, S. (1986) 'Independent living and the medical model of disability', *Disability, Handicap and Society*, **1** (2), 173–8.

Broadcasting Standards Council (1994) *Code of Good Practice*, 2nd edn, BSC, London.

Burleigh, M. (1994) *Death and Deliverance: Euthanasia in Germany 1900–1945*, Cambridge University Press, Cambridge.

Bury, M. B. (1982) 'Chronic illness as biographical disruption', *Sociology of Health and Illness*, **4** (2), 167–92.

Bury, M. B. (1996) 'Defining and researching disability: challenges and responses', in Barnes, C. and Mercer, G. (eds) *Exploring the Divide: Illness and disability*, The Disability Press, Leeds.

Campbell, F. (1981) 'Reviews: images of ourselves', in *In From the Cold*, first issue, June, The Liberation Network of People with Disabilities, London.

Campbell, J. and Oliver, M. (1996) *Disability Politics: Understanding Our Past, Changing Our Future*, Routledge, London.

Campling, J. (1979) *Better Lives for Disabled Women*, Virago, London.

Campling, J. (1981) *Images of Ourselves: Women with Disabilities Talking*, Routlege & Kegan Paul, London.

Chappell, A. (1992) 'Towards a sociological critique of the normalization principle', *Disability, Handicap and Society*, **7** (1), 35–52.

Coleridge, P. (1993) *Disability, Liberation and Development*, Oxfam Publications, Oxford.

Cook, J. and Mitchell, P. (1982) *Putting Teeth in the Act: A History of Attempts to Enforce the Provisions of Section 2 of the Chronically Sick and Disabled Persons Act 1970*, RADAR, London.

Coote, A. (1992) Introduction in Coote, A. (ed.) *The Welfare of Citizens: Developing New Social Rights*, Rivers Oram Press, London.

Craig, G. and Mayo, M. (1995) *Community Empowerment: a Reader in Participation and Development*, Zed Books, London.

Crow, G. (1997) *Comparative Sociology and Social Theory*, Macmillan, Basingstoke.

Cumberbatch, G. and Negrine, R. (1992) *Images of Disability on Television*, Routledge, London.

DAA (1995) 'Australia's northern territories pass euthanasia law' and 'China's eugenic policies', *Newsletter Twenty Eight*, Disability Awareness in Action, London.

Dalley, G. (1988) *Ideologies of Caring: Rethinking Community and Collectivism*, Routledge, London.

Darke, P. (1994) 'The elephant man (David Lynch, EMI Films): an analysis from a disabled perspective', *Disability and Society*, **9** (3), 327–42.

Daunt, P. (1991) *Meeting Disability: A European Response*, Cassell, London.

Davidson, F. W. K., Woodill, G. and Bredberg, B. (1994) 'Images of disability in 19th century British children's literature', *Disability and Society*, **9** (1), 33–47.

Davis, K. (1986) *Developing our own Definitions – Draft for Discussion*, British Council of Organisations of Disabled People, London.

Davis, K. (1990) 'Old medicine is still no cure', *Community Care*, 3 September.

Davis, K. (1993) 'The crafting of good clients', in Finkelstein, V., French, S. and Oliver, M. (eds) *Disabling Barriers – Enabling Environments*, Sage in association with the Open University, London.

Davis, K. (1994) 'Disability and legislation', in French, S. *On Equal Terms*, pp. 238–56, Butterworth-Heinemann, Oxford.

Davis, K. (1996) 'Disability and Legislation: rights and equality', in Hales, G. (ed.) *Beyond Disability: Towards an Enabling Society*, Sage, London.

Davis, K. and Mullender, A. (1993) *Ten Turbulent Years: A Review of the Work of the Derbyshire Coalition of Disabled People*, Nottingham, University of Nottingham, Centre for Social Action.

Davis, L. (1995) *Enforcing Normalcy: Disability, Deafness and the Body*, Verso, London.

De Jong, G. (1983) 'The movement for independent living: origins, ideology and implications for disability research', in Brechin, A., Liddiard, P. and Swain, J. (eds) *Handicap in a Social World*, pp. 239–48, Hodder & Stoughton in association with the Open University, Milton Keynes.

Despouy, L. (1993) *Human Rights and Disability*, United Nations Economic and Social Council, New York.

Dickel, D. N. and Doran, G. H. (1989) 'Severe neural tube defect syndrome from the early archaic of Florida', *American Journal of Physical Anthropology*, **80**, 325–34.

DIG (1965) The Memorandum and the Case Submitted by the Disablement Income Group (DIG) (to the Rt Honourable Mr Douglas Houghton, MP, Chancellor to the Duchy of Lancaster) Disablement Income Group, London.

Douglas, M. (1966) *Purity and Danger*, Routledge & Kegan Paul, London.

Doyle, N. and Harding, T. (1992) 'Community care: applying procedural fairness', in Coote, A. (ed.) *The Welfare of Citizens: Developing New Social Rights*, Rivers Oram Press, London.

DPI (1982) *Disabled People's International: Proceedings of the First World Congress*, Disabled People's International, Singapore.

DPI (1994) Agreed Statement at Human Rights Plenary Meeting in support of European Day of Disabled Persons, Disabled Peoples International, London.

Dreidger, D. (1989) *The Last Civil Rights Movement*, Hurst, London.

DS (1996) Special Issue: *Disability and Development Disability and Society*, **11** (4).

DSS (1994) *A Consultation on Government Measures to Tackle Discrimination Against Disabled People*, HMSO, Bristol.

Dugdale, R. L. (1877) *The Jukes: A Study in Crime, Paulerism, Disease and Heredity*, Putnam, New York.

Eldridge, J., Kitzinger, J. and Williams, K. (1997) *The Mass Media and Power in Modern Britain*, Oxford University Press, Oxford.

Ellis, K. (1993) *Squaring the Circle*, Joseph Rowntree, York.

ENIL (1989) *Press Release: European Network on Independent Living*.

EOC (1991) *Women and Men in Britain: A Statistical Profile*, Equal Opportunities Commission, London.

Esping-Andersen, G. (1990) *The Three Worlds of Welfare Capitalism*, Polity Press, Cambridge.

Evans, J. (1993) 'The role of centres for independent/integrated living' in *Making Our Own Choices; Independent Living, Personal Assistance and Disabled People*, pp. 59–63, The British Council of Organisations of Disabled People, Derby.

Fagan, T. and Lee, P. (1997) 'New social movements and social policy: a case study of the disability movement', in Lavalette, M. and Pratt, A. (eds) *Social Policy: A Conceptual and Theoretical Introduction*, Sage, London.

Featherstone, M., Hepworth, M. and Turner, B. (eds) (1991) *The Body: Social Process and Cultural Theory*, Sage, London.

Fiedler, B. (1988) *Living Options Lottery: Housing and Support Serices for People with Severe Physical Disabilities*, Prince of Wales Advisory Group on Disability, London.

Fiedler, L. (1981) *Pity and Fear: Images of the Disabled in Literature and the Popular Arts*, International Centre for the Disabled, New York.

Finch, J. (1986) *Research and Policy: The Uses of Qualitative Methods in Social and Educational Research*, Falmer Press, Sussex.

Fine, M. and Asch, A. (eds) (1988) *Women with Disabilities: Essays in Psychology, Culture and Politics*, Temple University Press, Philadelphia.

Finkelstein, V. (1980) *Attitudes and Disabled People: Issues for Discussion*, World Rehabilitation Fund, New York.

Finkelstein, V. (1991) 'Disability an administrative challenge: the health and welfare heritage?' in Hales, G. (ed.) *Beyond Disability: Towards an Enabling Society*, Sage, London.

Finkelstein, V. (1996) 'Outside inside out' in *Coalition Manchester*, pp. 30–6, Greater Manchester Coalition of Disabled People, Manchester.

Finkelstein, V. and Stuart, O. (1996) 'Developing new services', in Hales, G. (ed.) *Beyond Disability: Towards an Enabling Society*, Sage, London.

Foucault, M. (1977) *Discipline and Punish: The Birth of the Prison*, Allen Lane, London.

Friedmann, J. (1992) *Empowerment: The Politics of Alternative Development*, Blackwell, Oxford.

Galton, F. (1869) *Hereditary Genius: Its Laws and Consequences*, Macmillan, London.

Garland, R. (1995) *The Eye of the Beholder: Deformity and Disability in the Graeco-Roman World*, Duckworth, London.

Garland-Thompson, R. (1997) *Extraordinary Bodies: Figuring Physical Disability in American Culture and Literature*, Columbia University Press, New York.

Gartner, A. and Joe, T. (eds) (1987) *Images of the Disabled: Disabling Images*, Praeger, New York.

George, V. and Wilding, P. (1994) Welfare and Ideology, Harvester Wheatsheaf, London.

Gething, L. (1997) 'Sources of double disadvantage for people with disabilities living in remote and rural areas of New South Wales, Australia', *Disability and Society*, **12** (4), 513–33.

Giddens, A. (1994) *Beyond Left and Right: The Future of Radical Politics*, Polity Press, Cambridge.

Gillespie-Sells, K. and Campbell, J. (1991) *Disability Equality Training*, Central Council for the Education and Training of Social Workers, London.

Goddard, H. H. (1912) *The Kalikak Family: A Study in the Heredity of Feeblemindedness*, Macmillan, London.

Goffman, E. (1961) *Asylums*, Penguin, Harmondsworth.

Goffman, E. (1968) *Stigma: Notes on the Management of Spoiled Identity*, Penguin, Harmondsworth.

Gramsci, A. (1971) *Selections from the Prison Notebooks*, Lawrence & Wishart, London.

Green, D. (1993) *Reinventing Civil Society*, Institute for Economic Affairs, London.

Griffiths, R. (1988) *Community Care: Agenda for Action*, HMSO, London.

Hafferty, F. E. and Foster, S. (1994) 'Deconstructing disability in the crime mystery genre: the case of the invisible handicap', *Disability and Society*, **9** (2), 185–206.

Haffter, C. (1968) 'The changeling: history and psychodynamics of attitudes to handicapped children', *European Folklore Journal of the History of Behavioural Sciences*, **4**, 55–61.

Hahn, H. (1985) 'Disability policy and the problem of discrimination', *American Behavioural Scientist*, **28** (3).

Hahn, H. (1986) 'Public support for rehabilitation programmes: the analysis of US disability policy', *Disability, Handicap and Society*, **1** (2), 121–38.

Hanks, J. and Hanks, L. (1980) 'The physically handicapped in certain non-occidental societies', in Phillips, W. and Rotenberg, J. (eds) *Social Scientists and the Physically Handicapped*, Arno Press, London.

Hansard (1992) 31 January.

Harris, A. (1971) *Handicapped and Impaired in Great Britain*, HMSO, London.

Harrison, J. (1987) *Severe Physical Disability*, Cassell, London.

Harrison, P. (1992) *The Third Revolution*, Tauris, London.

Hastings, J. (ed.) (1918–1921) *Encyclopaedia of Religion and Ethics Vol. 5*, T. & T. Clarke, Edinburgh.

HCIL (1990) *HCIL Working Papers*, Hampshire Centre for Independent Living, Hampshire.

Hellender, E. (1993) *Prejudice and Dignity: An Introduction to Community Based Rehabilitation*, World Health Organisation, Geneva.

Hellender, E., Mendis, P., Nelson, G. and Goerdt, A. (1989) *Training the Disabled in the Community*, World Health Organisation, Geneva.

Hevey, D. (1992) *The Creatures Time Forgot: Photography and Disability Imagery*, Routledge, London.

Hills, J. (1995) *The Future of Welfare: A Guide to the Debate*, Joseph Rowntree Foundation, York.

Hirst, M. and Baldwin, S. (1995) *Unequal Opportunities: Growing up Disabled*, York University, Social Policy Research Unit, York.

HMSO (1989) *Caring for People*, HMSO, London.

Hobbes, T. (1983) 'Leviathan', in Held, D. (ed.) *States and Societies*, pp. 68–71, Martin Robertson, Oxford.

Hobsbawn, E. J. (1968) *Industry and Empire*, Penguin, Harmondsworth.

Hugman, R. (1991) *Power and the Caring Professions*, Macmillan, Basingstoke.

Humphries, S. and Gordon, P. (1992) *Out of Sight: The Experience of Disability 1900–1950*, Northcote House Publishers, Plymouth.

Hunt, P. (1966) 'A critical condition', in Hunt, P. (ed.) *Stigma: The Experience of Disability*, Geoffrey Chapman, London.

Hunt, P. (1981) 'Settling accounts with the parasite people', *Disability Challenge*, **2**, 37–50.

Hurst, R. (1995) 'International perspective and solutions', in Zarb, G. (ed.) *Removing Disabling Barriers*, Policy Studies' Institute, London.

Hyde, M. (1996) 'Fifty years of failure: employment services for disabled people in the UK', *Work, Employment and Society*, **12** (4), 683–700.

Ignatieff, M. (1989) 'Citizenship and moral narcissism', *Political Quarterly*, **60** (1), 63–74.

Independent Commission on Population and Quality of Life (1996) *Caring for the Future: Making the Next Decades Provide a Life Worth Living*, Oxford University Press, Oxford.

Inglis, F. (1991) *Media Theory: An Introduction*, Basil Blackwell, Oxford.

Ingstad, B. and Reynolds Whyte, S. (1995) *Disability and Culture*, University of California Press, Berkeley.

Irvine, J., Miles, I. and Evans, J. (1979) *Demystifying Official Statistics*, Pluto Press, London.

James, A. (1994) *Managing to Care*, Longman, Harlow.

Jones, K. and Fowles, A. (1984) *Ideas on Institutions*, Routlege & Kegan Paul, London.

Jones, K., Brown, J. and Bradshaw, J. (1983) *Issues in Social Policy*, 2nd edn, Routledge & Kegan Paul, London.

Keeble, U. (1979) *Aids and Adaptations*, Bedford Square Press, London.

Keep, J. and Clarkson, J. (1993) *Disabled People have Rights*, RADAR, London.

Keith, L. (1996) 'Encounters with strangers; the public's response to disabled women and how this affects our sense of self', in Morris, J. (ed.) *Encounters with Strangers*, Women's Press, London.

Keith, L. and Morris, J. (1996) 'Easy targets: a disability rights perspective on the "disability rights perspective"', in *Encounters with Strangers*, Women's Press, London.

Kestenbaum, A. (1993) *Making Community Care a Reality*, The Independent Living Fund, Nottingham.

Kestenbaum, A. (1995) *Independent Living: A Review*, Joseph Rowntree Foundation, York.

Kevles, D. J. (1985) *In the Name of Eugenics*, Alfred A. Knopf, New York.

Kitzinger, J. (1993) 'Understanding AIDS: media messages and what people know about AIDS', in Eldridge, J. *Getting the Message*, Routledge, London.

Kitzinger, J. (1995) 'The face of AIDS', in Marcova, J. and Farr, R. *Representations of Health and Illness*, Harwood Academic Publishers, London.

Knight, R. and Warren, M. (1978) *Physically Handicapped People Living at Home: A Study of Numbers and Needs*, HMSO, London.

Lakey, J. (1994) *Caring about Independence: Disabled People and the Independent Living Fund*, Policy Studies Institute, London.

Lamb, B. and Layzell, S. (1994) *Disabled in Britain: Counting on Community Care*, Scope, London.

Lees, S. (ed.) (1992) *Disability Arts and Culture Papers*, Shape Publications, London.

Leonard, P. (1997) *Post-modern Welfare: Reconstructing an Emancipatory Project*, Sage, London.

Levitas, R. and Guy, W. (eds) (1996) *Interpreting Official Statistics*, Routledge, London.

Lewis, A. (1995) *Children's Understanding of Disability*, Routledge, London.

Liggett, H. (1988) 'Stars are not born: an interpretive approach to the politics of disability', *Disability, Handicap and Society*, **3** (3), 263–76.

Lonsdale, S. (1990) *Women and Disability*, Macmillan, London.

Lukes, S. (1973) *Emile Durkheim: His Life and Work: A Historical and Critical Study*, Penguin, Harmondsworth.

Martin, J. and White, A. (1988) *The Financial Circumstances of Disabled Adults*, HMSO, London.

Martin, J., Meltzer, H. and Elliot, D. (1988) *OPCS Surveys of Disability in Great Britain: Report 1* – The Prevalence of Disability among Adults, HMSO, London.

Martin, J., White, A. and Meltzer, H. (1989) *Disabled Adults: Services, Transport and Employment*, OPCS, London.

Marx, K. (1970) *Capital Vol. 1*, Lawrence & Wishart, London.

Mason, M. (1992) 'Internal oppression', in Rieser, R. and Mason, M. *Disability Equality in the Classroom: A Human Rights Issue* (first published in 1990 by the ILEA), Disability Equality in Education, London.

Mason, P. (1997) Personal Communication, 10 November.

Meltzer, H., Smyth, M. and Robus, N. (1989) *Disabled Children: Services, Transport and Education*, HMSO, London.

Miles, I. and Irvine, J. (1979) 'The criticism of official statistics', in Irvine, J., Miles, I. and Evans, J. *Demystifying official statistics*, Pluto Press, London.

Miller, E. J. and Gwynne, G. V. (1972) *A Life Apart*, Tavistock, London.

Ming Guo (1993) 'Demographic features of people with disabilities in China', *Disability, Handicap and Society*, **8** (2), 207–10.

Morris, J. (1989) *Able Lives: Women's Experience of Paralysis*, Women's Press, London.

Morris, J. (1990) *Our Homes, Our Rights: Housing, Independent Living and Physically Disabled People*, Shelter, London.

Morris, J. (1991) *Pride Against Prejudice*, Women's Press, London.

Morris, J. (1993) *Independent Lives*, Macmillan, Basingstoke.

Morris, J. (ed.) (1996) *Encounters with Strangers: Feminism and Disability*, Women's Press, London

Murphy, R. (1987) *The Body Silent*, Henry Holt, New York.

NCIL (1997) Personal communication, 24 September, National Centre for Independent Living, London.

Nicholli, O. (1990) 'Menstruum quasi monstruum; monstrous births and menstrual taboo in the sixteenth century', in Nuir, E. and Ruggiero, G. (eds) *Sex and Gender in Historical Perspectives*, Johns Hopkins University Press, Baltimore.

Norden, M. (1994) *The Cinema of Isolation*, Rutgers University Press, New Jersey.

Norwich, B. (1994) *Segregation and Inclusion: English LEA Statistics 1988–92*, Bristol Centre for Studies on Inclusive Education, Bristol.

Norwich, B. (1997) *A Trend Towards Inclusion*, Centre for Studies on Inclusive Education, Bristol.

Offe, C. (1984) *Contradictions of the Welfare State*, Hutchinson, London.

Oliver, M. (1983) *Social Work with Disabled People*, Macmillan, Basingstoke.

Oliver, M. (1987) 'Redefining disability: some implications for research', *Research, Policy and Planning*, **5**, Spring, 9–13.

Oliver, M. (1990) *The Politics of Disablement*, Chapter Two, Macmillan and St Martins Press, Basingstoke.

Oliver, M. (1991) 'Disability and participation in the labour market', in Brown, P. and Scase, R. (eds) *Poor Work*, Open University Press, Milton Keynes.

Oliver, M. (1994) 'Capitalism and ideology: a materialist critique of the normalization principle', paper given at International Conference 'Normalization: 25 years on', Ottawa, Canada.

Oliver, M. (1996) *Understanding Disability: From Theory to Practice*, Macmillan, Basingstoke.

Oliver, M. and Barnes, C. (1993) 'Discrimination, disability and welfare: from needs to rights', in Swain, J., Finkelstein, V., French, S. and Oliver, M. (eds) *Disabling Barriers – Enabling Environments*, Sage in association with the Open University, London.

Oliver, M. and Barnes, C. (1997) 'All we are saying is give disabled researchers a chance', *Disability and Society*, **12** (5), 221–40.

Oliver, M. and Hasler, F. (1987) 'Disability and self-help: a case study of the Spinal Injuries Association', *Disability, Handicap and Society*, **2** (2).

Oliver, M. and Zarb, G. (1989) 'The politics of disability: a new approach', *Disability, Handicap and Society*, **4** (3), 11–14.

Oliver, M. and Zarb, G. (1992) *Personal Assistance Schemes; An Evaluation*, Greenwich Association of Disabled People, London.

Oliver, M., Zarb, G., Silver, J., Moore, M. and Sainsbury, V. (1988) *Walking into Darkness: the Experience of Spinal Cord Injury*, Tavistoch, London.

Pagel, M. (1988) *On Our Own Behalf; An Introduction to the-Self-organisation of Disabled People*, GMCDP Publications, Manchester.

Parker, I. (1995) 'Spitting on charity', *The Independent on Sunday: Sunday Review*, 9 April, p. 6.

Parsons, T. (1951) *The Social System*, Free Press, New York.

Pfeiffer, D. (1994) 'Eugenics and disability Discrimination', *Disability and Society*, **9** (4), 481–500.

Pfeiffer, D. (1997) 'The Americans with Disabilities Act: an examination of compliance by state, territorial and local governments in the USA', *Disability and Society*, **12** (5), 753–74.

Philips, V. (1993) *Caring for Severely Disabled People: Care Providers and their Costs*, Independent Living Fund, Nottingham.

Potts, M. and Fido, R. (1991) *A Fit Person to be Removed: Personal Accounts of Life in a Mental Deficiency Institution*, Northcote House, Plymouth.

Potts, P. (1989) 'Working report: educating children and young people with disabilities or difficulties in learning in The People's Republic of China', in Barton, L. (ed.) *Integration: Myth or Reality*, Falmer Press, London.

Prescott Clarke, P. (1990) *Employment and Handicap*, Social and Community Planning Research, London.

Quicke, J. (1985) *Disability in Modern Children's Fiction*, Croom Helm, London.

RADAR (1993) *Disability and Discrimination in Employment*, Royal Association of Disability and Rehabilitation, London.

Radford, J. P. (1994) 'Intellectual disability and the heritage of modernity', in Rioux, M. H. and Bach, M. *Disability is not Measles*, Roeher Institute, York University, York.

Rae, A. (1990) Secretarial Address, BCODP Annual General Meeting and Conference, Nottingham University, 17 September, Nottingham.

Rasmussen, K. (1908) *People of the Frozen North*, Lipincott, Philadelphia.

Ratzka, A. (1992) 'Independent living', in *World Congress III: Disabled Peoples' Equalisation of Opportunities*, pp. 23–5, Disabled Peoples' International, Vancouver, Canada.

Rieser, R. (1992) 'Children's literature', in Rieser, R. and Mason, M. *Disability Equality in the Classroom: A Human Rights Issue* (first published in 1990 by the ILEA), Disability Equality in Education, London.

Rieser, R. and Mason, M. (eds) (1992) 'Disability culture', in *Disability Equality in the Classroom: A Human Rights Issue*, 2nd edn, pp. 61–78, Disability Equality in Education, London.

Rioux, M. H. and Bach, M. (1994) *Disability is Not Measles*, York University, Roeher Institute.

Rioux, M. H., Crawford, C., Ticoll, M. and Bach, M. (1997) 'Uncovering the shape of violence: a research methodology rooted in the experience of people with disabilities', in Barnes, C. and Mércer, G. *Doing Disability Research*, The Disability Press, Leeds.

RNIB (1990) *Thomas Rhodes-Armitage RNIB Founder*, Royal National Institute for the Blind, London.

Roth, M. and Kroll, J. (1986) *The Reality of Mental Illness*, Cambridge University Press, Cambridge.

Rothman, D. (1971) *The Discovery of the Asylum*, Little Brown, Boston.

Rowe, A. (ed.) (1990) *Lifetime Homes: Flexible Housing for Successive Generations*, Helen Hamlyn Foundation, London.

Ryan, J. and Thomas, F. (1987) *The Politics of Mental Handicap*, revised edn, Free Association Books, London.

Scheer, J. and Groce, N. (1989) 'Impairment as a human constant: cross cultural and historical perspectives', *Journal of Social Issues*, **44**, 23–37.

Scott Parker, S. (1989) *They Aren't in the Brief*, Kings Fund Centre, London.

Scull, A. (1984) *Decarceration*, 2nd edn, Polity Press, Cambridge.

Shakespeare, T. (1993) 'Disabled people's self-organisation: a new social movement?', *Disability, Handicap and Society*, **8** (3), 249–64.

Shakespeare, T. (1994) 'Cultural representations of disabled people: dustbins for disavowal', *Disability and Society*, **9** (3), 283–301.

Shakespeare, T. (1996) 'Disability, identity and difference' in Barnes, C. and Mercer, G. *Exploring the Divide*, The Disability Press, Leeds.

Shakespeare, T., Gillespie-Sells, K. and Davies, D. (1996) *The Sexual Politics of Disability*, Cassell, London.

Solecki, R. S. (1971) *Shanidar: The First Flower People*, Alfred A. Knopf, New York.

Stevenson, O. and Parsloe, P. (1993) *Community Care and Empowerment*, Joseph Rowntree Foundation, York.

Stone, D. (1985) *The Disabled State*, Macmillan, Basingstoke.

Stone, E. (1996) 'A law to protect: a law to prevent: contextualising disability legislation in China', *Disability and Society*, **11** (4), 469–87.

Stuart, O. (1992) 'Race and disability: what type of double disadvantage?', *Disability, Handicap and Society*, **7** (2), 177–89.

Sutherland, A. T. (1981) *Disabled We Stand*, Souvenir Press, London.

Swann, W. (1992) *Integration Statistics: English LEAs 1988–91*, Bristol Centre for Studies on Inclusive Education, Bristol.

Taylor, D. (ed.) (1996) *Critical Social Policy: A Reader*, Sage, London.

Thomas, A. P., Bax, M. C. O. and Smyth, D. P. L. (1989) *The Health and Social Needs of Young Adults with Physical Disabilities*, Blackwell Scientific Publications, Oxford.

Thomas, K. (1977) 'The place of laughter in Tudor and Stuart England', *Times Literary Supplement*, 21 January, 77–81.

Thornton, P. and Lunt, N. (1995) *Employment for Disabled People*, University of York Social Policy Research Unit, York.

Tomlinson, S. (1982) *A Sociology of Special Education*, Routledge & Kegan Paul, London.

Topliss, E. (1982) *Social Responses to Handicap*, Longman, Harlow.

Topliss, E. and Gould, B. (1981) *A Charter for the Disabled*, Blackwell, Oxford.

Tooley, M. (1983) *Abortion and Infanticide*, Oxford University Press, New York.

Townsend, P. (1967) *The Last Refuge*, Routlege & Kegan Paul, London.

Townsend, P. (1979) *Poverty in the United Kingdom*, Penguin, Harmondsworth.

Trevelyan, G. A. (1948) *English Social History*, Longmans Green, London.

Turner, V. (1967) *The Forest of Symbols: Aspects of Ndembu Ritual*, Cornell University Press, New York.

United Nations (1988) *A Compendium of Declarations on the Rights of Disabled Persons*, United Nations, New York.

UPIAS (1976) *Fundamental Principles of Disability*, Union of Physically Impaired Against Segregation, London.

Walker, A. (1982) *Unqualified and Underemployed*, Macmillan/National Children's Bureau, London.

Warburton, W. (1990) *Disability Services for Disabled People*, HMSO, London.

Weber, M. (1948) *From Max Weber: Essays in Sociology*, Edited with an Introduction by H. H. Gerth and C. Wright Mills, Routledge & Kegan Paul, London.

Wendell, S. (1996) *The Rejected Body: Feminist and Philosophical Reflections on Disability*, Routledge, London.

Wertheimer, A. (1988) *According to the Papers: Press Reporting on People with Learning Difficulties*, Values Into Action, London.

Wilde, O. (1966) *Complete Works*. Collins, London.

Williams, F. (1989) *Social Policy, a Critical Introduction: Issues of Class, Race and Gender*, Polity Press, Cambridge.

Wolfensberger, W. (1980) 'The definition of normalisation: update problems, disagreements and misunderstandings' in Flynn, R. J. and Nitsch, K. E. *Normalisation, Social Integration and Community Services*, MD University Park Press, Baltimore.

Wolfensberger, W. (1989) 'Human service policies: the rhetoric versus the reality', in Barton, L. (ed.) *Disability and Dependence*, Falmer, Lewes.

Wolfensberger, W. (1994) 'The growing threat to the lives of handicapped people in the context of modernistic values', *Disability and Society* **9** (3), 395–413.

Wood, P. (1980) *International Classification of Impairments, Disabilities and Handicaps*, World Health Organisation, Geneva.

Wood, R. (1990) 'Care of disabled people', paper presented at seminar entitled 'The needs and resources of disabled people', Policy Studies Institute, London, 3 December.

Zarb, G. (1995) 'Modelling the social model of disability', *Critical Public Health*, **6** (2), 21–9.

Zarb, G. (1997) 'Researching disabling barriers', in Barnes, C. and Mercer, G. (eds) *Doing Disability Research*, The Disability Press, Leeds.

Zarb, G. and Oliver, M. (1993) *Ageing with a Disability: What Do they Expect after All these Years?* University of Greenwich, London.

Zarb, G. and Nadash, P. (1994) *Cashing in on Independence: Comparing the Costs and Benefits of Cash and Services*, The British Council of Disabled People, Derby.

Zola, I. (1981) *Missing Pieces: A Chronicle of Living with Disability,* Temple University Press, Philadelphia.

INDEX